Interface Issues
An Annotated Bibliography

Mary Conway and Jonny Byrne

Institute for Conflict Research

First Published August 2005

Institute for Conflict Research
North City Business Centre
2 Duncairn Gardens
Belfast BT15 2GG
Tel: 028 9074 2682
Fax: 028 9035 6654
Email: info@conflictresearch.org.uk
www.conflictresearch.org.uk

Belfast Interface Project
Glendinning House
6 Murray Street
Belfast BT1 6DN
Tel: 028 9024 2828
Email: info@belfastinterfaceproject.org
www.belfastinterfaceproject.org

ISBN: 0-9541898-6-8

This research was funded through the IFI Community Bridges Programme.

All photographs by Frankie Quinn

Produced by:
three creative company ltd

Table of Contents

	PAGE
1. Ballynafeigh Community Development Association (1994) A Study of Attitudes to Community Relations in a Mixed Area of Belfast.	8
2. Ballymurphy Women's Centre (2004) Women on the Edge: Conference Report.	8
3. Basten, Anne and Lysaght, Karen (2003) Violence, Fear and 'the everyday': Negotiating Spatial Practices in the City of Belfast.	9
4. Belfast Interface Project: Chris O'Halloran, Peter Shirlow and Brendan Murtagh (2004) A Policy Agenda for the Interface.	10
5. Belfast Interface Project (1999) Inner East Outer West.	11
6. Belfast Interface Project (1998) Interface Communities and the Peace Process.	12
7. Belfast Interface Project (1998) Young People on the Interface.	13
8. Bill, Anne (2002) Beyond the Red Gauntlet.	14
9. Birrell, Derek (1994) Social Policy Responses to Urban Violence in Northern Ireland.	15
10. Boal, Frederick (1995) Shaping a City: Belfast in the Late Twentieth Century.	16
11. Boal, Frederick (1982) Segregating and Mixing: Space and Residence in Belfast.	18
12. Boal, Frederick; Murray, R.C. and Poole Michael (1976) Belfast: The Urban Encapsulation of a National Conflict.	20
13. Bollens, Scott A. (2000) On Narrow Ground: Urban Policy and Ethnic Conflict in Jerusalem and Belfast.	23
14. Bollens, Scott A. (1998) Urban Peace-Building in Divided Societies: Belfast and Johannesburg.	24
15. Boyes, Kevin and Quinn, Frankie (1994) Interface Images.	27
16. Bryan, Dominic and Jarman, Neil (1999) Independent Intervention: Monitoring the Police, Parades and Public Order.	27
17. Bryson, Lucy and McCartney, Clem (1994) Clashing Symbols? A Report on the Use of Flags, Anthems and Other National Symbols in Northern Ireland.	28
18. Buckley, Anthony D. and Kenney, Mary Catherine (1995) Urban Spaces, Violence and Identity in North Belfast.	29
19. Cadwallader, Anne (2004) Holy Cross: The Untold Story.	30
20. Community Dialogue (2001) North Belfast: Where Are We At?	32
21. Connolly, Paul and Maginn, Paul (1999) Sectarianism, Children and Community Relations in Northern Ireland.	32

22. Darby, John (1996) Intimidation and the Control of
    Conflict in Northern Ireland. 33
23. Doherty, Paul and Poole, Michael (1995) Ethnic
    Residential Segregation in Belfast. 34
24. East Belfast Community Development Agency (2001) Leading
    from Behind: An Agenda for Change in East Belfast. 36
25. Ellis, Geraint and McKay, Stephen (2000) City Management
    Profile Belfast. 37
26. Fay, Marie Therese; Morrissey, Mike; Smyth, Marie and Wong,
    Tracy (1999) The Cost of the Troubles Study. 38
27. Forthspring Inter-Community Group and Belfast
    Exposed (2001) The Hurt, the Peace, the Love and the War. 38
28. Gaffikin, Frank; McEldowney Malachy and Sterrett, Ken (2001)
    Remaking the City: The Role of Culture in Belfast, in Urban
    Planning and Cultural Inclusion: Lessons from Belfast and Berlin. 39
29. Gallagher, Ryan (ed) (2000) BT5: A Photographic Exploration
    of Identity by Young People in East Belfast. 40
30. Garvaghy Residents (1999) Garvaghy: A Community Under Siege. 41
31. Hall, Michael (ed) (2005) Finding Common Ground:
    An Exploration by Young People from Both Sides of the
    East Belfast Interface. 41
32. Hall, Michael (ed) (2004) Exploring the Marching Issue:
    Views from Nationalist North Belfast. 42
33. Hall, Michael (ed) (2003) Beginning a Debate:
    An Exploration by Ardoyne Community Activists. 43
34. Hall, Michael (ed) (2003) The East Belfast Interface (1):
    Lower Newtownards Youth Speak Out. 44
35. Hall, Michael (ed) (2003) The East Belfast Interface (2):
    Short Strand Youth Speak Out. 45
36. Hall, Michael (ed) (2003) It's Good to Talk: The Experiences
    of the Springfield Mobile Phone Network. 46
37. Hall, Michael (ed) (2002) Reuniting the Shankill: A Report on
    the Greater Shankill Community Exhibition and Convention. 47
38. Hall, Michael (ed) (2002) An Uncertain Future: An Exploration
    by Protestant Community Activists. 49
39. Hall, Michael (ed) (2001) Community Relations:
    An Elusive Concept. 50
40. Hall, Michael (ed) (2001) Young People Speak Out:
    Newhill Youth Development Team. 51
41. Hall, Michael (ed) (1999) Living in a Mixed Community:
    The Experiences of Ballynafeigh. 52
42. Hamilton, Michael (2001) Working Relationships: An Evaluation
    of Community Mobile Phone Networks in Northern Ireland. 54

43. Heatley, Colm (2004) Interface: Flashpoints in Northern Ireland. 55
44. Henry, Pat; Hawthorne, Isy; McCready, Sam and Campbell, Hugh (2002) The Summer of 2002: An evaluation of the impact of diversionary funding for work with young people in Belfast interfaces during the summer of 2002. 56
45. Hepburn, A.C. (1994) Long Divisions and Ethnic Conflict: The Experiences of Belfast. 56
46. Inter-Action Belfast (2004) Strategic Plan 2004-2007. 58
47. Jarman, Neil (2005) Demography, Development and Disorder: Changing Patterns of Interface Areas. 59
48. Jarman, Neil (2002) Managing Disorder: Responses to Interface Violence in North Belfast and to Public Disorder Related to Disputes over Parade Routes. 60
49. Jarman, Neil (1999) Drawing Back from the Edge: Community Based Responses to Violence in North Belfast. 62
50. Jarman, Neil (ed) (1997) On The Edge: Community Perspectives on Civil Disturbances in North Belfast June-September 1996. 63
51. Jarman, Neil and O'Halloran, Chris (2000) Peacelines or Battlefields? Responding to Violence in Interface Areas. 64
52. Keane, Margaret Christine (1985) Ethnic Residential Change in Belfast 1969-1977: The Impact of Public Housing Policy in a Plural Society. 65
53. Kuusisto-Arponen, Anna-Kaisa (2003) Our Places - Their Spaces. 66
54. Lenadoon Community Forum (2003) Lenadoon Community Forum, 1992-2002. 66
55. McEldowney, Malachy; Sterrett, Ken and Gaffikin, Frank (2001) Architectural Ambivalence: the Built Environment and Cultural Identity in Belfast. 69
56. Moore, Ruth and Smyth, Marie (1996) Two Policy Papers: Policing and Sectarian Division; Urban Regeneration and Sectarian Division. 68
57. Murtagh, Brendan (2002) The Politics of Territory: Policy and Segregation in Northern Ireland. 69
58. Murtagh, Brendan (1999) Community and Conflict in Rural Ulster. 71
59. Murtagh, Brendan (1995) Image Making Versus Reality: Ethnic Division and the Planning Challenge of Belfast's Peace Lines. 72
60. Murtagh, Brendan (1994) Ethnic Space and the Challenge to Land Use Planning: A Survey of Belfast's Peace Lines. 73
61. Neill, William J.V. (1998) Whose City? Can a Place Vision for Belfast Avoid the Issue of Identity? 75
62. Neill, William J.V. (1995) Lipstick on the gorilla? Conflict management, urban development and image making in Belfast. 76

63. North Belfast Community Action Project (2002)
    Report of the Project Team. ... 79
64. Northern Ireland Housing Executive (2000)
    The North Belfast Housing Strategy: Tackling Housing Needs. ... 81
65. Officer, David (2001) Towards a Community Relations Strategy
    for Donegall Pass. ... 82
66. Persic, Callie (2004) The State of Play. ... 83
67. Robinson, Peter (2002) Victims: The Story of Unionists 'Living'
    at the Interface with Republican Short Strand. ... 85
68. Shirlow, Peter (2001) Fear and Ethnic Division. ... 85
69. Shirlow, Peter (1998) Fear, Mobility and Living in the Ardoyne
    and Upper Ardoyne. ... 86
70. Shirlow, Peter; Murtagh, Brendan; Mesev, Victor and McMullan, A.
    (2002) Measuring and Visualising Labour Market and
    Community Segregation: A Pilot Study. ... 89
71. Springfield Inter-Community Development Project (2000)
    The Feud and the Fury. ... 89
72. Springfield Inter-Community Development Project (1998)
    Report of a Series of Seminars. ... 90
73. Springfield Inter-Community Development Project (1993)
    Life on the Interface. ... 91
74. Smyth, Marie (ed) (1996) Life in Two Enclave Areas in
    Northern Ireland. ... 92
75. Smyth, Marie (ed) (1996) Public Discussions on Aspects
    of Sectarian Division in Derry Londonderry. ... 93
76. Smyth, Marie (1995) Three Conference Papers on Aspects
    of Segregation and Division. ... 94
77. Smyth, Marie (1995) Borders Within Borders: Material and
    Ideological Segregation as Forms of Resistance and Strategies
    of Control. ... 95
78. Smyth, Marie; Morrissey, Mike and Hamilton, Jennifer (2001)
    Caring Through the Troubles: Health and Social Services in
    North and West Belfast. ... 96
79. Todd, Helen (2002) Young People in the Short Strand Speak Out. ... 97
80. Williams, Sue and Williams Steve (2002) Ardoyne Road Arbitration:
    Report and Recommendations. ... 99
81. Woodvale Resource Centre (1998) Report on the
    Ardoyne-Springfield Interface. ... 100
82. Working Group on Peacelines (1994) Report. ... 101

Publications in Chronological Order ... 102
Index ... 107
ICR Reports ... 108

Preface

Belfast Interface Project (BIP) is a membership organisation committed to informing and creating effective regeneration strategies in Belfast's interface areas.

Much has been written about interface areas and issues by researchers, academics, community and statutory agencies and others. This body of work represents a considerable store of knowledge and experience, insight, theory and opinion in this area, gathered over many years. One of the aims of BIP is to enhance and develop the knowledge base regarding Belfast's interface areas. In order to facilitate this process of knowledge development, it seemed appropriate to commission the Institute for Conflict Research to bring together within one document a collection of abstracts of existing literature.

This document represents an attempt to make this body of literature more accessible to those who may be interested in this area, including our members and key stakeholders. The collection of abstracts document is indexed by author, chronology and theme and is also available for download from our website at www.belfastinterfaceproject.org.

Accompanying this document, BIP has brought together a library of hard copies of the source materials summarised within it. This library is housed in our offices and is available to BIP members and key stakeholders.

We aim, over future years, to regularly update both the collection of abstracts document and the library of source materials as new literature is added.

We hope you find this resource relevant and useful.

Chris O'Halloran
Director, Belfast Interface Project.

Introduction

Security barriers and interface communities are a result of ongoing community conflict and tension in Northern Ireland. Research shows that interface communities have suffered a disproportionately high level of violence and disorder during the Troubles. Although progress has been made through paramilitary ceasefire and political agreements, it is now estimated that communities are more tightly defined and defended than at any other time in history. The creating of barriers to limit contact between feuding communities has had limited success, as inter-communal violence has persisted even after the construction of a barrier. There are currently 27 Northern Ireland Office built walls, fences or barriers, which mark the boundaries between Protestant/Unionist and Catholic/Nationalist communities in Belfast, with a further 10 in other areas of Northern Ireland.

While some interface areas have recorded low levels of violence and disorder in recent years, other areas have witnessed an increase in community violence and segregation. Tensions have risen and violence has threatened to engulf numerous interface communities each year. These inter-communal hostilities can be attributed to political, parade, protest or policing decisions and activities. However, it is feared that low-level sectarian violence has become a permanent backdrop to daily life within interface areas. The cost of this violence and segregation manifests itself through high poverty rates, low levels of educational attainment, an inability to access resources and feelings of threat and besiegement. Understanding and addressing these concerns may encourage resolutions which lower communal tensions, prioritise shared concerns and promote economic regeneration in both interface areas and across Northern Ireland.

This annotated bibliography is a compilation of research on interface issues and areas, which has been undertaken by voluntary agencies, academic institutions, research organisations and community forums. This publication provides a resource for individuals interested in the dynamics of interface communities, aims to assist researchers in their studies on Belfast interfaces, and allows for comparisons to be drawn between research findings. The study aims to disseminate good practice policies, research findings, successful ventures and community viewpoints to interested parties across Northern Ireland.

This report reflects the authors' interpretations of the provided material. It does not necessarily directly reflect the perspectives presented in each publication.

1. **Ballynafeigh Community Development Association (1994)** *A Study of Attitudes to Community Relations in a Mixed Area of Belfast.* **Belfast, Ballynafeigh Community Development Agency.**

This report examines attitudes towards community relations in the mixed Ballynafeigh community of Belfast. The research specifically questions the attractiveness of mixed areas, and examines the extent to which 'mixing' between Protestant and Catholic residents occurs. The report traces the historical concept of community relations in Belfast, and concludes that Ballynafeigh is not socially engineered as a mixed community. The research examines ongoing attempts to enhance community relations within the community. The social and economic diversity within this community is also presented and discussed.

The attitudes of Ballynafeigh residents regarding sectarian tensions and political affiliations are compared to the Northern Ireland Attitudes Survey findings and the Northern Ireland 1991 census. The Ballynafeigh survey addresses residential demographics, religious composition, attitudes towards living in a mixed community, attitudes towards policing, the impact of political violence upon Ballynafeigh and political affiliations. The research finds overwhelming support for living in and maintaining the mixed area. The study confirms the research hypothesis that Ballynafeigh is a mixed area currently undergoing change and is currently experiencing low levels of stress and sectarian tension.

2. **Ballymurphy Women's Centre (2004)** *Women on the Edge: Conference Report.* **Belfast, Ballymurphy Women's Centre.**

This document outlines the discussion topics raised during the 'Women on the Edge' conference. The forum was open to all women from Nationalist areas across Northern Ireland, and included many personal accounts of interface conflict. The workshop sessions discussed many important and interlinked themes regarding community isolation, policing, violence, and political representation. Personal safety issues featured prominently among respondents, with many discussing their inability to access local services because of real and perceived intimidation. The main concerns surrounded media bias, education systems, grievances towards the PSNI, housing demands and political isolation.

The conference called for a zero-tolerance policy towards all sectarian attackers and abusers to be adopted by government and statutory agencies. The participants also endorsed recognition of human rights and called for the end of media sensationalism. It was recommended that the legal system classifies all sectarian crimes as hate crimes, and prosecute offenders accordingly. The group called on the DHSS and all Heath Trusts to ensure services remain available to all communities throughout the year, and the Education Service to maintain a long-term approach for children living in violent areas. The forum recommended that the Housing Executive review current policies regarding housing and availability.

3. **Basten, Anne and Lysaght, Karen (2003) Violence, Fear and 'the everyday': Negotiating Spatial Practices in the City of Belfast. In Elizabeth Stanko (ed) *The Meaning of Violence.* London, Routledge.**

This paper examines violence, segregation and the spatialised nature of fear in Northern Ireland. The report observes how one act of sectarian violence affects community-wide perceptions of safety and danger. This perception of a relative threat informs decisions on spatial behaviour and creates various coping strategies. The paper concludes that residential movements are a behavioural response to violence, and that the recent rise in violence has increased overall community fear regarding spatial relations.

The research scrutinises the daily negotiation of spatial practice, and evaluates various coping strategies. It also examines the existing paradox of residents of working class communities, who admit to little contact with the other community but demonstrate detailed knowledge of one another. It finds that ritualised acts of conflict between neighbouring districts have reinforced community identities. Through these interactions, local residents lose anonymity and become known to their assailants. The paper evaluates the various coping strategies employed by residents to conceal ethnic identity. Restraints on clothing, language, and group size are discussed. These restrictions result from a fundamental need to avoid provoking a negative reaction from the other community. The paper concludes that residents regulate their behaviour to reduce provocation and predictability and to best manage their identity in hostile areas.

The paper also examines the notion of shared space beyond residential boundaries, and concludes that space outside residential areas is equally segregated. The marching season increases tensions and imposes further restrictions on movement. The repercussions of sectarianised space are found to be particularly significant to those without private

transportation. The research concludes that spatial practices are rule-bound and imposed to minimise risk. These geographic divisions extend into neutral space, and both communities defer to these boundaries, while spatial divisions are maintained in order to regulate usage of shared space and conceal community identity.

4. Belfast Interface Project: Chris O'Halloran, Peter Shirlow and Brendan Murtagh (2004) *A Policy Agenda for the Interface.* **Belfast, BIP.**

This report calls for a concerted, integrated, well-funded long-term strategy to address the ongoing problems within Belfast's interface areas. The report categorises previous government interface policies as crisis support rather than strategic planning. The multiple deprivations suffered by interface communities across North Belfast are discussed. The report describes the interconnected nature of fear, economic decline and environmental problems, which have hindered interface regeneration. The available evidence indicates a distinct sense of local territorial control, avoidance and segregation. The report also provides a detailed description of the attitudes held by interface residents regarding deprivation, spatial interaction and sectarian violence. This research measures the effect of the 1994 paramilitary ceasefires and subsequent peace agreements on the economic and social conditions of interface communities and specifically discusses the impact of spatial segregation upon available employment. Local perceptions of violence and antisocial behaviour are also included.

Previous government policies directed towards interface areas are reviewed and the report analyses primary, secondary and community-centred interface policies. These policies contain specific goals for interface areas, such as the absence of violence, strong community infrastructure, collective community activism, community leadership, political support, paramilitary engagement and support, and the appropriate role of non-governmental organisations. The report concludes by providing further recommendations for a variety of statutory and government agencies, while maintaining that interface development requires substantial funding and planning initiatives.

5. Belfast Interface Project (1999) *Inner East Outer West*. Belfast, BIP.

This booklet outlines the recent successes of inter-community contact between Short Strand and Inner East and the Suffolk and Lenadoon communities. The term Inner East was coined to describe the 'peace lines' that mark the boundaries of the Catholic Short Strand enclave and the neighbouring Protestant communities in Inner East Belfast. The reference to Outer West denotes the 'peace lines' that define the boundaries between the Protestant Suffolk estate and the neighbouring Catholic areas. This booklet examines the process by which local activists have confronted issues of violence and division between the communities. The first two sections contain case studies of each community, and the final section discusses shared difficulties of cross-community participation.

The first study summarises numerous interviews with community activists representing the Suffolk and Lenadoon communities. This cross-community work was intended to address local concerns, interface issues and reservations regarding the 'other' community. The group eventually came together once community tensions had subsided. Both the larger Suffolk and Lenadoon communities were supportive of this contact and agreed with plans for local economic regeneration. The community activists discussed possible initiatives to reduce local tension and violence. Working together with residents groups, community activists issued statements condemning all forms of violent protests throughout the summer marching season. Additionally, group members began using a mobile phone network, and monitored interfaces to defuse riotous situations. While these measures dramatically reduced interface violence, high levels of tension and fear remained between the communities.

The second study examines the ongoing attempts to ease sectarian tension and violence around the inner east interface. The early work involved encouraging young people away from interface areas to reduce the potential for hostile situations. The group leaders broadened their membership to promote local community development and continue cross-community dialogue. Group members initiated a mobile phone network, which subsequently defused interface tensions. The association continued to prioritise their agenda over the winter months, and surveyed local residents about community concerns. The survey work was finished before the contentious summer marching season and community activists patrolled interfaces, pulled back hostile groups and defused rumours. While sporadic violence continues to occur, activists feel larger incidents involving larger groups of rioters have noticeably declined.

The study identifies shared concerns between community members, namely interface violence, young people, building cross-community relations and economic regeneration. Cooperation produced positive results, such as a reduction in inter-community violence, local regeneration and increased communication and understanding between community leaders, along with a relative reduction in community tension. All areas faced difficulties in accessing local facilities, high levels of economic and social deprivation, and intra-community tensions. The research concludes that enclave areas are both symptoms and symbols of political and cultural interaction. These outside issues affect community activist's abilities to engage in intercommunity dialogue. Fear of retribution from within one's community remains a major barrier to intercommunity dialogue. According to this report, intercommunity work can be a difficult but ultimately rewarding process, which can subsequently create momentum for future progress.

6. **Belfast Interface Project (1998)** *Interface Communities and the Peace Process.* Belfast, BIP.

This brief publication discusses the primary concerns of interface communities and puts forward several key recommendations for practical confidence-building measures to address interface apprehension regarding the peace process. The research defines the appearance, existence and numbers of interfaces that currently exist across Northern Ireland. Three types of interface communities, enclave areas, buffer zones and split areas, are identified and analysed. The research identifies the rationale for the continued existence of interfaces as providing physical protection, psychological security and solidarity. The multiple disadvantages suffered by interface communities are also discussed.

The study prioritises several aspects of socio-economic concerns for interface areas, identified as the needs of children and young people, the effects of violence, restrictions on travel and access to facilities, and participation of young people in inter-community violence. The study goes on to emphasise the importance of support and leadership, to create and increase community infrastructure. Maintaining this programme would enable communities to address issues of concern and possibly facilitate communication between interface areas.

The report calls on government leaders to address interface issues in order to restore faith and stabilise societies most harmed by ongoing violence. Five recommendations, all themed as confidence-building measures, are put forward in the report. These call for financial assistance and support of local measures aimed at reducing interface violence and tensions, while focusing on the specific needs of children and young people; promoting economic and environmental regeneration of interface 'wasteland' areas, and assisting in the process of healing and coping with traumas.

7. **Belfast Interface Project (1998)** *Young People on the Interface*. Belfast, BIP.

Young People on the Interface examines the role of children and young people as both victims and perpetrators of interface violence and the subsequent stigmatisation in local media outlets and government publications. The research argues that, in order to break the cycle of inter-communal mistrust, division and violence, it is necessary to recognise and address the needs of those affected by and socialised into the cycle. The publication identifies the shared levels of economic and social disadvantage, ongoing levels of violence and restricted access to facilities that harm all interface communities.

The interviews include a specific section discussing the methodology and interview process used during the research. It was found that the young people interviewed were not stereotypical troublemakers, but ordinary young people growing up with an unusual combination of factors that affected their lives.

The research found that religious affiliation made little difference when it came down to how young people identified issues that concerned them in their everyday lives. On the topic of social activities, it was found that young people were dissatisfied with youth club offerings and were seen as a nuisance when gathered on streets or street corners. Interfaces were found to be attractive gathering spots, away from community supervision. Varied responses were given for participation in youth-inspired violence but overall findings suggested excitement and 'buzz' from participation, rather than a desire to destroy an enemy. Interface violence was found to be ritualistic in nature, with strong adherence to unwritten rules. The effects of violence were found to generate general fear and apprehension in respondents. Notably, concern was expressed related to one's 'own' community reaction towards cross-community socialisation. Some young people believed that community divisions were insurmountable, while others remained more optimistic.

The perceptions of youth workers are also included to supplement young people's views. Both intra-community and inter-community divides were discussed. However, intra-community violence was found to fade in comparison to the inter-community situation. The youth workers identified interface areas as 'magnets' for crowds of young people. Participation in interface violence was found to link young people to their communities, through their actions 'defending' the area. Programmes developed for the summer of 1997 demonstrated to Belfast youth workers that it is possible to impact and lessen street conflict. Some youth workers reported that interface violence could be switched on and off by community elements. The youth workers also identified a positive sense of self-awareness in the interface youths.

It was found that young people remain alienated from their own community and the police. A difficult relationship exists between young people and local paramilitaries. The stark levels of limitations placed upon young people, along with inadequate youth provision, has increased the attractiveness of interface violence. In terms of the way forward, the research identified further research, increased community provision and community-led intervention as imperative. The research identified a need for intra-community dialogue and single-identity work for young people before embarking upon cross-community dialogue.

8. Bill, Anne (2002) *Beyond the Red Gauntlet*. Belfast, AB Publications.

This book presents a specific Unionist perspective on the Holy Cross conflict. The motivation for the protest is portrayed as drawing attention to community safety concerns, and not specifically targeting school pupils. The first chapters describe the violent incidents that sparked the school protest and conclude that long-standing community intimidation and lack of government resources left the Upper Ardoyne community feeling alienated and deprived.

The author includes personal accounts of sectarian violence within the community. A number of topics are covered in the book including the Concerned Residents of Upper Ardoyne efforts to quell the crisis, and the community's difficulties in engaging in meaningful dialogue with their Catholic counterparts during the summer. The author also indicates that police aggression transformed a peaceful protest into a violent confrontation.

Since the cessation of the Holy Cross protest, the author alleges that violent attacks against Upper Ardoyne residents have increased. The book includes many firsthand accounts from local residents, discussing their fear of violent attacks and their anger regarding the inability of local government and police to protect their community.

9. Birrell, Derek (1994) Social Policy Responses to Urban Violence in Northern Ireland. In Seamus Dunn (ed) *Managing Divided Cities*. Keele, Ryburn Publishing.

This chapter analyses the specific policies implemented to offset continuing violence and instability in Northern Ireland. The first section, *Constraints on Social Policy Responses*, identifies the parity principle that attempts to keep Northern Ireland's social policies in uniformity with Great Britain, which leaves little opportunity for distinctive social policy initiatives. Northern Ireland has not escaped from pressure to reduce public expenditure, overall public expenditure per capita has been nearly 40 percent higher in Northern Ireland than Great Britain. The majority of this funding targets law and order and industrial development, yet Northern Ireland still reports higher levels of social deprivation than any other UK region. The system of local government has few responsibilities regarding the delivery of social policies, which makes participation by local representatives difficult and the co-ordination of services problematic.

Section Two: *Responses to Acute Urban Deprivation* discusses the multiple initiatives designed to tackle acute social deprivation in Northern Ireland. It has long been noted that Northern Ireland is the least prosperous UK region, and has high levels of poverty, unemployment, and welfare dependency. The section identifies Making Belfast Work as an agenda of extra funding to tackle problems of unemployment, poor educational achievement and poor health in the disadvantaged areas of Belfast. The authors indicate that Making Belfast Work has not been very successful in providing employment, but has had success with community-based clubs and training schemes. The Londonderry Initiative was established as an equivalent to Making Belfast Work, but was more focused on various aspects of urban decline within the Derry region; it successfully encouraged private sector investment within the local area. Finally, the section discusses the Community Economic Regeneration Scheme, which provides opportunities for urban communities to become involved in the development and ownership of major economic assets in local areas. The chapter concludes by providing several criticisms of these government-funded programmes.

Section Three: *Responses to Inequalities Between Communities* identifies discrimination in housing and employment as a major factor in civil disturbances. The creation of the Northern Ireland Housing Executive was intended to introduce affordable housing and end housing shortages. The authors credit the Housing Executive with removing politics from housing and ending sectarian discrimination in housing. According to the research, religious discrimination in employment has continued. The section traces the legislation and authoritative bodies established to address this problem, which remain committed to affirmative action as opposed to quotas or reverse discrimination. This section also examines a number of deep structural reasons to explain the continuing employment imbalance.

Section Four: *Responses to Community Division* examines government policies created to address community partition and evaluates the different levels of government funding for segregated schools, employment and deprived areas. The study provides several reasons for increased residential segregation, including fear, intimidation and personal preference. The research finds no existing government policy designed to address increasing residential segregation or maintain existing integrated areas.

Section Five: *Responses to Physical Violence* addresses the lack of academic research regarding policy response to direct violence. The research illustrates the numerous statutory agencies which fall into the category of emergency planning, but also maintain significant social policy aspects. These schemes provide social assistance for both property destruction and personal injuries. The study indicates a direct correlation between social deprivation and violence.

10. Boal, Frederick (1995) *Shaping a City: Belfast in the Late Twentieth Century.* **Belfast, Institute of Irish Studies.**

Shaping a City plots the growth and development of Belfast over the past thirty years. The study examines how the city and surrounding areas have been affected by economic, ethno-national and demographic change, through words, graphs, maps and photographs.

Chapter One: *When and Where - From the Beginning to the 1960s* traces the growth of Belfast and examines major historical events which gave Belfast its unique character. The rise of Belfast as a significant settlement is attributed to the 17th century plantation of Ulster. The industrial growth of the city encouraged migration and recorded significant growth in the Catholic population. The research correlated a rise in Catholic/Protestant friction to a similar rise in economic expansion.

Chapter Two: *Population since the 1960s* measures the city population and spatial distribution as key indicators of urban change and tension. The study examines three rings of urbanisation: the City Centre, Commuter Settlements and the Inner Core City. In the years 1971-1991, the study recorded a dramatic decline in core city population, with equally dramatic growth in the outer reaches of the regional city. The research identifies an overall decline in household size, with sharp rises in single-person and elderly households. The study identifies a contradictory phenomenon of declining city population, along with an increasing demand for dwelling units. Belfast is attributed with rising levels of segregation over the past thirty years, characterised by tranquil periods, when segregation remains static or declining, followed by inter-communal conflict and corresponding segregation increases. Each conflict has led to new and higher levels of segregation, classified by the research as the 'segregation ratchet'. Although segregation is found in both working-class and middle-class communities, the research identifies stronger levels of segregation in working-class areas.

Chapter Three: *The Planning Experience* identifies three basic themes that dominated Belfast Urban Planning. The need to limit the physical build-up of the urban areas by limiting outward growth has been on the agenda for a long period of time. Additionally, the need to amend poor housing conditions in the Inner Core City, and the preservation of agricultural zones have influenced planning decisions. The research finds that little was done to amend these concerns until the 1960s, when city planners prioritised the management of growth. The study examines the turbulent events of the 1970s, and concludes that urban planners were hindered by demographic, economic and ethnic problems.

Chapter Four: *Housing the People* discusses the improvements to public sector dwellings over the past thirty years. The study details the high levels of unfit housing and massive renovation projects undertaken by the NIHE. The research also examines the multiple problems encountered by the NIHE during the renewal process. A subsequent rise in owner-occupied properties is recorded. The housing revolution was most evident in the inner city, where residents were able to access financial assistance for home renovation. The study provides in-depth analysis of current Protestant / Catholic dwelling locations, and concludes that the Protestant community has access to a wider range of suburban housing options, and subsequently migrated from the Belfast Urban Area.

Chapter Five: *In and Out of Work* identifies community conflict, associated violence and unemployment as dominant influences over

Belfast residents during the past thirty years. The study finds the same patterns of disadvantage in the inner city and western sector dating back to 1974. Along with the loss of manufacturing jobs, the research identifies ethnic segregated geography as hindering employment.

Chapter Six: *Special Places: Lagan Corridor and City Centre* examines the role and development of the Lagan riverside and City Centre within the Belfast Urban Area. The history of the Lagan and special provisions to protect environmentally friendly areas are discussed. The transformation of the City Centre from target of urban terrorism to economic powerhouse is included. The research tracks the remarkable recovery of the City Centre during the 1980s-1990s and credits the Urban Development Grant as providing primary assistance to the project.

Chapter Seven: *Sustainable City* defines sustainable development as a kind of development that meets the needs of the present without compromising the ability or resources of future generations. The section includes a history of Belfast public transport and the role of the Black Taxi service and the heavy reliance on private cars. The study calls for future policy that emphasises public transport, walking and cycling. The research goes on to define Belfast urban sustainability as recognition of cultural, social and ecological concerns. The study concludes that Belfast has battled between sustainability and unsustainability over the past thirty years. In terms of environmental concerns, Belfast remains far from sustainable.

11. Boal, Frederick (1982) Segregating and Mixing: Space and Residence in Belfast. In Frederick Boal and Neville Douglas (eds) *Integration and Division: Geographical Perspectives on the Northern Ireland Problem.* **London, Academic Press.**

This article examines the degree to which ethnic residential segregation exists in Belfast by exploring patterns of residential integration. The article begins by presenting numerous theories relating to residential segregation and cultural assimilation, and classifies Northern Ireland as characterised by both cultural and structural pluralism. Boal's research argues that, when a high degree of residential segregation exists, assimilation will be limited, as physical separation enhances differences and division. The chapter measures the extent to which residential segregation has existed in Belfast at different times and considers any temporal variations which have occurred.

Section One: *Ethnic Segregation in Belfast Over Time* suggests residential segregation has been a feature of Belfast since its inception. The chapter

notes growing segregation and physical hostilities during the 19th century. The research examines residential data from 1911, 1969 and 1972, and concludes that residential segregation has sharply increased during this time period.

Section Two: *Ethnic Residential Mixing* establishes a degree of residential mixing as a fixed feature in Belfast. The study uses maps to establish the fixed locations of mixed communities.

Section Three: *Households in Mixed Streets* considers the theory that mixed areas tend to contain a majority of Protestant households and a minority of Roman Catholic households. The research establishes a housing division between predominantly occupied 'non-manual' and 'manual' households. Owner occupied homes are classified in the 'Upper' category, and distinctions are made between the rental sector as 'Lower Private' and public housing as 'Lower Public'. The ethnic make up of a mixed area is classified into three categories, Protestant large majority, Protestant small majority and Catholic majority.

Section Four: *Perceptions of Neighbourhood Ethnic Change* finds that ethnically mixed areas which are stable tend to establish a degree of permanence, while transitioning mixed areas suggest impermanence. It is found that stable areas are more likely to reduce inter-ethnic differences. The research questions Upper, Lower Private and Lower Public residents about perceptions of ethnic makeup in their area.

Section Five: *Analysis of Localities* examines mixed housing groups in specific spatial locations and finds distinctive patterns of movement in each case-study area.

Section Six: *Further Aspects of Mixing* identifies three factors that directly affect mixing and assimilation as: length of residence in current address, age of head of household, and temporal perspective. The research concludes that many mixed areas in Belfast cannot be viewed as stable units of ethnic integration. The dynamic of ethnic residential segregation in Belfast in 1970 was found to be producing more mixed areas. However most of this mixing only occurred in the short term, as the 'invaded' group tended to move away.

Section Seven: *Discussion* identifies ethnic residential mixing as limited in nature and dependent upon social class and dwelling characteristics. The article makes four observations regarding factors which influence residential mixing.
- Middle class areas tend to be less ethnically segregated than their working-class counterparts.
- A greater degree of conflict exists between ethnic groups in working-class areas.
- The most marked change in ethnic composition has occurred and is occurring in certain segments of the Lower Private housing category.
- Protestant households form substantial majorities in most mixed-street situations.

The article concludes that ethnic segregation has long been a feature of Belfast. The mixing which has occurred tends to be in middle-class areas. The research argues that mixed areas are vulnerable to destabilisation from ethnic conflict outbursts. Boal concludes that mixing will only lead to assimilation in well-established stable areas.

These findings are also published in:
Boal, Frederick (1969) Territoriality on the Shankill-Falls Divide. *Irish Geography; Dublin Geographical Society* Vol. 6, No. 1.
Boal Frederick (1971) Territoriality and Class: A Study of Two Residential Areas in Belfast. *Irish Geography; Dublin Geographical Society* Vol. 6 No. 3.

12. Boal, Frederick; Murray, C. and Poole, Michael (1976) Belfast: The Urban Encapsulation of a National Conflict. In Susan Clark and Jeffrey Obler (eds) *Urban Ethnic Conflict: A Comparative Perspective.* Chapel Hill, University of North Carolina.

This publication examines the basis for ethnic residential segregation in Belfast, and seeks to contradict the class interpretation of the Belfast conflict. The study begins by arguing that the conflict in Belfast can only be understood if viewed in both ethnic group terms and national terms, and concludes that residential segregation remains a key measurement of the level and intensity of conflict.

Section One: *Introduction* traces the legacy of residential segregation to the early 17th century and argues that the partition of Ireland was the outcome of growth of two distinct Irish nations, each with independent culture, religion, identity and perceptions of history. This lack of identifiably national or ethnic homogeneity within Northern Ireland has led to modern-day urban segregation in Belfast.

Section Two: *The 'Two Nations'* concludes that the conflict in Northern Ireland, particularly in Belfast, is an ethnic conflict, due to the strength and continuity of different national aspirations. The study found little to no interaction between groups, which enhances inter-group conformity and increased distance between factions. The polarised social structure in Belfast was not supportive of claims that conflict within Belfast is based on social-class conflict.

Section Three: *Historical Overview of Ethnic Conflict in Belfast* identifies residential segregation as existing from the founding of the city. The effects of sectarian intimidation have spurred housing shifts from both communities. These periodic disturbances between Catholics and Protestants have sharpened residential segregation and have provided a physical manifestation of the conflict.

Section Four: *The Function of Ethnically Segregated Residential Areas* identifies ethnic segregation as common in all ethnic conflict situations. Residential clusters were identified as serving defensive and conservative functions against outside pressure, with four specific purposes:
- **Defensive Functions** concludes that single-identity areas provide a simplistic defensive arrangement for minority groups, which typically maintain homogeneous ethnic characteristics. Segregation often enables organisation and defence to develop within an area.
- **Avoidance Functions** speculates that segregated areas provide psychological relief against unfamiliarity.
- **Preservative Functions** theorises that single-identity areas successfully preserve and promote a distinct cultural heritage. This section also addresses the value and importance placed on segregated education.
- **Attack Functions** describes the ability to maintain a safe and supportive basis for urban guerrilla warfare.

Section Five: *Territory* describes the fundamental importance of ethnic residential concentrations across Belfast territory. The different perceptions of working-class and middle-class residents towards segregation are noted. The section explores the relevance of parades and violence regarding shifting ethnic demographics.

Section Six: *The Conflict-Segregation Relationship* examines the necessity of ethnic residential segregation for personal security. The study concludes that when the sense of threat (either real or perceived) escalated, residential segregation sharply increased.

Section Seven: *Residential Segregation in Belfast* identified 70% of Belfast residents as living in single-identity areas. The research measures the dimensions of ethnicity and social class upon living arrangements in Catholic cities, Protestant cities and mixed cities. It was reported that segregation was higher for the working-class. Residential segregation was found to have increased since the start of the modern Troubles. It was found that 23% of Belfast Urban Area households had shifted in the years between 1969-1973. Notably, most of these relocations occurred during the summer months. Catholics were found more likely to relocate than their Protestant counterparts.

Section Eight: Segmented City and Community Action measured a low level of inter-ethnic social interaction within Belfast, which created the socially and spatially fragmented city. This separation supported the emergence of community self-management within highly segregated ethnic areas, as an extension of functions of typical ethnic residential areas under extreme duress.

Section Nine: The 'Class Conflict' and 'Relative Deprivation' Perspectives finds it unlikely that class-conflict interpretation could explain the Catholic-Protestant Belfast conflict. The research conducted a thorough examination of distribution through the housing system, and found that Catholics have greater access to public housing, while Protestants are more present in the private rented sector. Each group was found to access different geographical segments of the housing market. The two ethnic groups have access to separate segments of the education service, reinforcing overall geographic segregation. Although the research rejects class interpretations of the Belfast conflict, it concludes that national conflict has a high manifestation within working-class areas through residential segregation and perpetuation of violence.

Section Ten: Conclusions deduces that initial Belfast segregation is a reflection of underlying national conflict, and that increases in segregation correspond to escalation of conflict. The continuity of ethnic-national conflict can be explained by the ever-present 'national' question. The research places Belfast in the middle of the British/ Irish interface zone, and attributes residential segregation as a critical mechanism for group survival. The study concludes by dismissing antisegregationist arguments as counter-productive, and calls for a shift in emphasis acknowledging the positive functional aspects of urban ethnic residential segregation.

13. Bollens, Scott (2000) *On Narrow Ground: Urban Policy and Ethnic Conflict in Jerusalem and Belfast.* **Albany, State University of New York Press.**

This book explores the ways in which urban policy is affected by deep-rooted nationalistic conflict and how local decisions affect the dynamic of the conflict. The work identifies cities as capable of exerting independent effects on ethnic tensions, conflict and violence, and examines the effects of urban policymaking on ethnic relations and political settlements. The study links the conflict in Belfast to the maintenance of ethnic territory and identity, which government 'colour neutral' policies fail to address.

The study begins by examining the numerous obstacles created by sectarianism, territoriality and peace barriers in Belfast, and the approaches taken by urban policymakers to address these problems. The study finds that the priorities of urban policymakers, namely maintaining neutrality and assuring ethnic stability, have subsequently perpetuated community divisions and created financially impractical solutions.

The research then examines government involvement in project-based changes to the urban landscape and explores the tactics used to overcome sectarian complexities. The research focuses on the Northern Ireland Housing Executive policies on integration, segregation and 'colour-blind' allocations. Bollens finds that NIHE has no existing coherent, strategic, citywide approach towards the sectarian realities in Belfast. The research suggests that city centre investments and Making Belfast Work projects have failed to stem economic disadvantage in Belfast's deprived areas.

The study finds that 'policy neutral' positions create unequal outcomes, poor public acceptance and ineffectiveness in addressing deprivation. Instead, the study finds a need for more explicit accounting of ethnic factors in planning and development decisions. Case studies from Yorkgate shopping centre, Springvale, the Central Community Relations Unit and Making Belfast Work are discussed. Bollens finds that neutral policy is not receptive to different community concerns, yet colour-perceptive policies may be influenced by sectarian politics. The study concludes that urban policy has a responsibility to facilitate and enable the co-existence and viability of both Protestant and Catholic communities in Belfast.

14. Bollens, Scott (1998) *Urban Peace-Building in Divided Societies: Belfast and Johannesburg.* Oxford, Westview Press.

Chapter Four: *The Sectarian City:* examines different aspects of conflict in Belfast, and identifies obstacles that hinder cross-community relationships. Belfast is identified as a stage upon which a broad national conflict is performed. This conflict has been exacerbated because religious identities coincide with strong political and national loyalties. The research examines the 'double-minority' syndrome on the island and effects on leadership and peace-building. The research cites the three linked phenomena of suburban stagnation, loss of core city population and urban fringe growth as causing rapid spatial transformation near Belfast city centre. The chapter finds that the city geography both reflects and intensifies spatial conflict.

The chapter documents how Direct Rule was brought in during 1972 to combat discrimination in the Northern Ireland parliament and make Northern Irish civil servants accountable to Westminster MPs. It concludes that the Northern Ireland Assembly is the first, but not a completely sufficient, mechanism to normalise Northern Irish society. The research further predicts that this form of government will produce insurmountable gridlocks.

Recent population trends have produced densely populated and active Catholic neighbourhoods and lower-density, socially deplete and physically deteriorated Protestant neighbourhoods. The construction of 'peace lines' was found to maintain community perceptions of security in the middle of a civil war. The study concludes that the biggest problem for urban policymakers is that they are put in the political hot seat when deciding the future of under-utilised Protestant communities. The publication includes case studies from the Suffolk Estate and Cluan Place, and concludes that 'peace lines' are not a cause of conflict, but a reflection of urban geography that is overwhelmed by fear and territoriality.

Bollens assesses the economic conditions in Belfast and Northern Ireland and shows reliance upon public sector money and substantial resources allocated for law and order. He emphasises the need to address deprivation and unemployment across Northern Ireland, but questions community leadership and priorities. The study discusses the growth of different types and objectives of community groups from the 1970s until present day and examines the difference between Protestant and Catholic community organisation, and current political splits within each community. The chapter concludes by examining the obstacles to in-depth cross-community work.

Chapter Five: *British Urban Policy Since 1972:* examines the various approaches that Belfast urban policymakers have taken towards the realities and challenges of sectarianism. Bollens finds that the government objectives of maintaining comprehensive strategies for urban betterment are contradicted by necessary strategies for urban security. Over the past twenty-five years, urban policy in Belfast has erred towards maintenance, security and neutrality, which illustrates the government's acceptance of the conflict. Although integration is promoted by various planning agencies, planning organisations are unable to force social engineering. The section concludes that government stance is based upon not disturbing the delicate territorial balance in the city.

He describes the development of sectarian territory, and government acceptance of the demarcations. The research explains how population changes have affected planning decisions, and explores the relationship between sectarianism and the allocation of public housing. The NIHE's policy of 'colour-blind' housing allocation is found to reproduce sectarian geography. A case study of the Catholic Poleglass estate is included, which shows how the NIHE addresses Belfast sectarian geography. Belfast urban policy is found to be spread across numerous organisations, without a coherent policy for addressing sectarianism. The study finds that this method denies comprehensive land planning, and provides urban planners with a reactive, rather than proactive policy. The research concludes that developmental institutions, such as the NIHE and Belfast Development Office, are not guided by a coherent city-wide approach, and therefore approach problems in a vertical and single-function manner, rather than laterally and coordinating across functions.

Bollens argues that a neutral policy of allocation in an unequal society results in unequal opportunities. A case study of the NIHE allocation scheme highlights the unequal system. The study suggests that monitoring and allocation by religion would illuminate unequal outcomes and help design corrective policy. It is suggested that more urban planning funds are directed towards safer, neutral areas, rather than divided communities. The study shows that the economic growth of these areas hardly benefits deprived communities. The research concludes that many neutral policies often perpetuate social and economic inequalities and are incapable of addressing the unique needs of either community.

Chapter Six: *Belfast and Peace:* analyses contemporary urban policy in Belfast, and argues that the policy-neutral position has failed to address the complexities of ethnic compartmentalization. The study examines alternative approaches to Belfast urban policy, and outlines a proactive role for Northern Ireland government in dealing with ethnic issues, which falls between a passive reflection of need and aggressive social engineering. It argues that single issue-based interventions into city building and planning have ignored the complex reality of sectarian geographies. Instead, urban planning must ensure co-existent viability of all sides in the urban system, by openly accounting for all ethnic factors in planning and government decisions. The section challenges government officials to address sectarian considerations and redefine planning functions beyond traditional roles, while encouraging a multidimensional approach to ethnic management. This progressive ethnic strategy would engage multiple government units laterally, rather than the current non-integrated approach.

The specific problems of targeting disadvantaged areas in a polarised city are discussed, as one community would tend to receive more resources than the other. Belfast's history of refusing to spatially target community deprivation is discussed, along with the city's current reliance upon the Making Belfast Work programme and concludes that Belfast's urban policy has separated political allegiances from socio-economic needs. Bollens examines the plausibility of going beyond quantifiable need by examining and working towards community regeneration goals. The difficulties surrounding interface housing stock and population trends are discussed. The section concludes that a citywide urban planning strategy must identify and prioritise viable communities in order to appropriately target resources to areas capable of recovery.

Bollens emphasises the need for an urban policy that is sensitive to the unique needs of each community, while keeping in mind the overall good of the city. He argues that urban policy should not force integration, but facilitate it in more stable areas and concludes that the Northern Ireland Housing Executive and government should pursue more open strategies, while enunciating the advantages of an urban strategy of co-existent viability to Protestant and Catholic communities. The current policy of neutrality is identified as reinforcing sectarian divisions, and instead the goal that the government should strive for is the viability of the two communities. The chapter concludes that Belfast Urban Strategy should not remain colour neutral, but sensitive to the different needs of the two communities. A strategy based on colour where colour matters, instead of neutrality, would contribute to peacemaking.

15. Boyes, Kevin and Quinn, Frankie (1994) *Interface Images*. Belfast, Belfast Exposed Community Photography Group.

This book contains a number of striking interface pictures from across Belfast. The book's introduction contains a brief outline of the origins of peacelines in Northern Ireland. The main part of the book is a number of photographs that capture the deprivation and ongoing sectarian tension within Belfast's interface communities.

16. Bryan, Dominic and Jarman, Neil (1999) Independent Intervention: Monitoring the Police, Parades and Public Order. Belfast, Democratic Dialogue and Community Development Centre.

The research focuses on the creation of civil society groups willing to observe, monitor and possibly intervene in events. An analysis of the range of organisations and multiple objectives is included. The report aims to unravel the complexities of monitoring groups and the diversity of approaches, aims and practices. It establishes the theoretical contexts and various approaches to monitoring and defines monitors as organisations that principally observe and record events. The difficulties of monitoring, namely the validity of recorded responses and inability to view entire events are discussed. The importance of domestic monitoring groups, which are available to monitor events on a more permanent basis, are considered and case studies of domestic monitoring schemes are included. The research finds that the presence of observers can decrease violence, but observers can do little to amend basic injustices.

The study examines groups that intend to monitor for potential and/or actual abuse of human rights while focusing on the relationship between police and demonstrators. The research examines groups that make active choices to ensure peaceful outcomes and maintain public order. Mediators are attributed with successfully decreasing violence at contentious events, and make themselves available should problems develop between key players. Community-Based Activity is defined by the study as community initiatives to defuse local tensions and prevent violence, and where members remain willing to intervene on the ground and actively try to maintain the peace. Such groups typically intervene between one party and the police, rather than between two other conflicted parties, and the organizations do not claim to be inpendent or impartial.

The final section identifies three beneficial types of monitoring in Northern Ireland, namely human-rights monitors, community-based monitors and stewards. The research concludes that maintaining public order is not simply a policing problem, but a responsibility of civil society and includes general recommendations for different types of monitoring group.

17. Bryson, Lucy and McCartney, Clem (1994) *Clashing Symbols? A Report on the Use of Flags, Anthems and Other National Symbols in Northern Ireland.* Belfast, Institute for Irish Studies/Community Relations Council.

Clashing Symbols examines the controversial and divisive nature of specific flags, anthems and other items in Northern Ireland. The study presents a comparative explanation that combines historical, anthropological, legal and other perspectives to obtain and understand community attitudes.

Chapter One: *Flags and Anthems in a Global Context* presents various theories explaining the popularity of certain flags and anthems. The chapter traces the historical development of flags across several case studies, along with examining emotional responses to certain flags. The increase of flags in Northern Ireland over recent years is cited as a cultural and social phenomenon.

Chapter Two: *British and Irish Symbols and Their Significance* provides an overview of flags which are important to different Northern Irish communities. The chapter notes the shades of opinions and perceptions within each community towards Unionist and Nationalist principles. The research found asymmetrical views between the communities regarding symbols: the Unionist sense of self required self-expression through flags, bunting and anthem displays, while the Nationalist sense of identity existed regardless of physical demonstration. The research concludes that each side did not see that they were complaining about behaviour by the other community which was similar to how they behaved themselves.

Chapter Three: *Special Occasions and Social Institutions* discusses the presence of flags and the singing of anthems during certain times of the year. The research found that individuals were prepared to tolerate behaviour in their own tradition, which they would not tolerate in those from another tradition.

Chapter Four: *Symbols in Everyday Community Life* examines the informal use of flags in local communities, as this form of individual behaviour is not regulated by any official body. It examines two case studies regarding Twelfth decorations and Irish-language street signs. The research found that specific forms of display have changed, but that the meaning and impact associated with certain symbols have intensified. As each group has felt more challenged, there has been a stronger need to assert group identity. The section examines the role of flags and anthems in inciting hatred and increasing local tensions.

Chapter Five: *National Symbols, The Community and Public Order* traces the history of displaying flags and emblems before the partition of Ireland and examines the effects of the Flags and Emblems (Display) Act 1954 in Northern Ireland.

Chapter Six: *National Symbols in the Work Place* reveals the historical presence of flags and bunting in factories and offices and provides certain case studies describing the contentious use of flags in mixed-religion workplaces. The chapter concludes with a case study of restrictions and identity displays in the Northern Ireland prison service.

The publication concludes that there is no standard approach towards flags and symbols, and presents several options for the Northern Irish legislature. The research considers potential ways of using flags and anthems to satisfy identity desires by non-controversial means. The study examines the right to freedom of expression in Northern Ireland, and concludes that voluntary restraints on freedom of expression are unlikely to be sufficient.

18. **Buckley, Anthony and Kenney, Mary Catherine (1995) Urban Spaces, Violence and Identity in North Belfast. In Buckley, Anthony and Kenney, Mary Catherine** *Negotiating Identity: Rhetoric, Metaphor and Social Drama in North Belfast.* **Washington, Smithsonian Institution.**

This chapter demonstrates the influence of historical settlement patterns upon violence and ethnicity in Northern Ireland by conducting a detailed analysis of the Ardoyne community. The research classifies Belfast as an urban system that continually regenerates sectarian distinctions and indicates that the fierce sectarianism found in working-class Belfast communities has subsequently stressed rural divisions.

Section One: *Historical Dimensions of Urban Territory* traces interface rioting back to the nineteenth century. The research finds that early riots were related to major political interests of the day along with annual festivals. When violence began in 1969, it assumed nineteenth-century riot patterns, but the research concludes that riots now occur along new interfaces created by Catholic expansion across urban Belfast.

Section Two: *Ardoyne and its Boundaries* examines the violent history of the Ardoyne-Woodvale interface. In the past, residents living in local mixed areas retreated to the safety of their heartland communities. The residential relocation has increased segregation between communities and hardened interface boundaries.

Section Three: *At the Border* discusses the sense of besiegement that saturates Ardoyne. Although the research identifies current riots as recreational in nature and primarily undertaken by young people, there is an indication that these violent actions have serious consequences, which contribute to the chronic sense of being under threat. The section provides a detailed account of the events between August 9-11th 1986, and the subsequent deterioration of the interface area.

Section Four: *The Republicans* discusses the high status awarded to members of the Provisional movement within Ardoyne society. The research examines the tenuous relationship between the Roman Catholic Church and paramilitary groups. The study finds that Republicans portray themselves as saviours of the local people, while community members fear local retribution for reporting criminal events to the police. The research examines the poverty and psychological stress within the area, and concludes that the sense of permanent threat provides the basis for passive support of the IRA. In conclusion, the chapter identifies the sense of besiegement as providing a basis for the acceptance of republican ideologies and practices.

19. Cadwallader, Anne (2004) *Holy Cross: The Untold Story.* Belfast, Brehon Press.

Holy Cross: The Untold Story pieces together perspectives of parents, children, politicians, protestors and police in an attempt to compile an account of the events surrounding the Holy Cross dispute. Cadwallader begins by examining the long history of violence and disorder in North Belfast, particularly between Catholic Ardoyne and Protestant Glenbryn. The start of the dispute is traced back to 1997, and the refusal of an extension to the Alliance Avenue peace line. This issue resurfaced in 2001, and played a prominent role in behind-the-scenes political negotiations during the protest. A tense atmosphere, enhanced by an alleged sectarian hit-and-run incident, initially triggered the Holy Cross protest. The research traces cross-community attempts to resolve local disorder before the Autumn 2001 Holy Cross school term. However, the ongoing violence across North Belfast, and the inability of the Right to Education group (RTE) to address concerns from the Concerned Residents of Upper Ardoyne (CRUA) led to protests along Ardoyne Road. Cadwallader presents firsthand accounts from parents, children, police and protestors during the school protest. CRUA are portrayed as having no coherent strategy or leadership for their protest. The daily levels of violence, abuse and tactics employed by the protestors are recorded.

Both parents and protestors were angered at the slow response time of politicians during the protest. The proposed alternative route to Holy Cross School is examined, and the research concludes that decisions to either walk through the protest or along the alternative route were made according to individual family desires. The research recounts the inability of police to control violence during the protest and between interface communities. Criticism regarding the policing of the protest is recorded from both sides. The book discusses the psychological impact of the protest upon the families and communities. Themes of stress, memory repression and increasing sectarian attitudes are discussed. The supportive role of Father Troy, Father Donegan and Holy Cross principal Anne Tanney as mediators and leaders is analysed. Cadwallader cites uneducated and inflammatory press coverage as harming the situation.

Cadwallader concludes that the Holy Cross protest exposed the weakness of the devolved power-sharing assembly. She concludes that the Holy Cross protest was unique amongst Northern Ireland's ethnic conflicts, because those involved consciously knew that children would suffer. Both communities united separately under the immense strain and the wish to avoid another protest. After examining recent attitudes in Ardoyne and Glenbryn, the book found a depressed atmosphere and an unwillingness to engage in cross-community activities. Cadwallader concludes that the protest demonstrates how far the North has to travel before becoming a normal society.

20. **Community Dialogue (2001)** *North Belfast: Where Are We At?* **Belfast, Community Dialogue.**

This leaflet poses a number of questions pertaining to the future of North Belfast raised by community and youth workers. A number of topics are explored, including housing, security, paramilitaries and young people. The publication emphasises the need for inclusive dialogue and the development of shared responses to difficulties.

21. **Connolly, Paul and Maginn, Paul (1999)** *Sectarianism, Children and Community Relations in Northern Ireland.* **Coleraine, Centre for the Study of Conflict.**

This research examines the impact of the Northern Ireland conflict on children, and the related emergence and development of prejudice. The study also offers a comprehensive analysis of previous methodology and provides a detailed rationale for the argument that an alternative methodological approach is necessary. The research examines the multiple definitions of sectarianism and argues that sectarianism is not simply distinguished though individual behaviours, but remains embedded within broader socio-cultural, political and economic structures.

Chapter Two: *Learning from Research on Children and Prejudice* acknowledges that research findings on sectarian experiences of children are limited. The study addresses the known facts about racial prejudice among children, and then assesses these in the context of Northern Ireland. The study concludes that children develop a rudimentary understanding of the concepts Catholic and/or Protestant and that this knowledge evolves with age and social interactions.

Chapter Three: *Research on the Contact Hypothesis* addresses the success of cross-community programmes and the effects of participation upon children. It concludes that participants of short-term contact programmes (such as mixed holidays) are likely to revert to their previous beliefs once they return to their original settings, and remain unlikely to change their long-term beliefs or attitudes.

Chapter Four: *Towards an Alterative Methodological Approach* presents a new and more inclusive method for studying sectarianism and community relations work, which focuses on the experience of children within a broad social context. This work advocates a more unstructured, qualitative methodology, which would permit children to talk openly and candidly about their own perspectives and experiences, therefore accommodating different social contexts and processes. The chapter discusses two key concerns regarding this approach, namely the ethics of interviewing children directly about sectarianism and the need for a correct interpretation of the collected data.

Chapter Five: *Sectarianism and Children's Perspectives* focuses on children's knowledge and understanding of the political situation in Northern Ireland. The research finds that perceptions of police do not mimic parental opinions, but were rooted in children's personal experiences. The study emphasises how children actively construct their own understandings of the conflict, rather than uncritically reproduce family views.

Chapter Six: *Children and Contact Schemes* draws upon a case-study of Protestant and Catholic children attending a cross-community disco. The research finds that this contact led to some of the participants reinforcing their existing sectarian beliefs. The study identified the disco as a main social context within the child's life. It was concluded that the disco was a risky setting to initiate cross-community contact, as status among peers was at stake, and the programme did not include any anti-sectarian work. This situation therefore helped to sustain and reinforce existing sectarian beliefs. A number of general recommendations conclude this research, many of which address the need to adapt research methodology to a more qualitative, ethnographic and contextual approach to better address children's own experiences and perceptions.

22. Darby, John (1996) *Intimidation and the Control of Conflict in Northern Ireland.* Syracuse, Syracuse University Press.

This book examines the historical nature of violence in Belfast, and concludes that all incidents of major rioting have emerged from a combination of political unrest and a particular cataclysmic incident. The study also addresses the Belfast housing 'separation' process during the mid 19th century. Darby argues that during periods of violence, the pressures to conform to one's co-religionists were much greater, and that strict partitions were quickly accepted. The study examines the importance of group identity and perceived threats. This perception subsequently creates strong group identification based on mutual contradictions and misunderstanding. This sense of threat would become heightened during periods of violence, and was stronger outside the most segregated areas rather than inside them.

The author identifies tangible differences between the two religious groups by citing examples of economic prosperity, demographic location, institutional arrangements and social relationships. Darby supports the theory of a direct link between deprivation and minority discontent. He also examines the widespread polarisation of schools, sports and leisure activities. The research identifies three factors which challenge the straightforward theory of Catholic/Protestant segregation; namely cross-community relationships, mutual deprivation and shifting allegiance.

The book contains three case studies of interface and enclave areas in Belfast. According to the findings, all three areas became more polarised in the periods following intimidation. A single incident of sectarian hostility was found to encourage residents' decisions to leave the area and secure a position within a religious 'heartland'. The predominant perception of single-identity areas reinforced an exterior sense of threat and besiegement. Darby concluded that geographical segregation and low levels of contact between protagonists enhance the potential for inter-community violence. Ethnic identities remain capable of being triggered by important events and while segregated living provides a measure of control over participation in and development of conflict, an increase in violence may draw outlying group members towards militarised positions.

23. Doherty, Paul and Poole, Michael (1995) *Ethnic Residential Segregation in Belfast*. **Coleraine, Centre for the Study of Conflict.**

This research examines the effects and boundaries of religious residential segregation in Northern Ireland. Previous research has acknowledged segregation as both a cause and consequence of violence. This study discusses the difficulty in distinguishing between 'voluntary' and 'involuntary' segregation in the context of Northern Ireland. While the research attributes a correlation between segregation and violence, it does not prove that the former causes the latter. The first chapter includes previous research that examined religious segregation and the shrinkage of mixed neighbourhoods.

Chapter Two: *The Historical Development of Segregation Up to 1935* details demographic changes in Belfast during the 19th century and their subsequent effects on politics, segregation and tension. The research argues that segregation increased in a series of spasmodic jumps: each time rioting broke out it would leap up, possibly falling back in a more peaceful interlude, but advancing every time violence renewed. The chapter ends by describing the violence of 1935, and concludes that this time-period (1896-1935) ended an era of massive sectarian conflict that had perpetuated the growth and development of a segregated city.

Chapter Three: *The Historical Development of Segregation: 1935 to the Present Day* examines the growth of the Catholic population in the Belfast urban areas during the mid-Twentieth century and the lack of sectarian violence. The chapter then highlights the beginning of violence and large-scale residential relocation between 1969-1972, which indicated a definitive increase in spatial polarisation. It is claimed that the housing system perpetuated this segregation, as new housing took on the ethnic demographics of neighbouring areas.

Chapter Four: *Segregation in Belfast 1971-1991: Some Methodological Issues* discusses the difficulties of relying on census data and focuses on the non-statement of religion, the under-enumeration of the population and the struggle to apply consistent solutions/amendments to the missing data. The researchers decide to measure segregation only between stated Catholics and the remaining population.

Chapter Five: *Ward Level Segregation* analyses residential segregation based on the 15-ward system and concludes that, even at a very simple level of spatial segregation patterns, substantial evidence demonstrates patterns of separate living by the two communities. In total, 47.4% of the Belfast population live in highly segregated wards.

Chapter Six: *Segregation at the Grid Square Level* examines the overall population decline of the city of Belfast, and illustrates how the Catholic population of the urban areas rose from 27.4% (1971) to 31.2% (1991). The researchers summarise these findings by concluding that suburbs have become more Protestant, while the urban areas have become more Catholic. The public sector housing market, it is argued, has perpetuated the desire for segregated communities.

Chapter Seven: *Religion as an Ethnic Indicator* details several formulations which would assist researchers in filling missing census data. After a review of all available solutions, the authors conclude that both No Religion and Not Stated groups are primarily Protestant, but that in west Belfast both groups are primarily Catholic.

Chapter Eight: *Summary and Conclusions* reviews the focus on the relationship between residential segregation and violence. Three important findings have been developed from this research. First, segregation in Belfast has been in existence since the origins of the city. Secondly, segregation is

the spatial outcome of violence. Thirdly, the overall trend in segregation, as proven by the data analysis, is upward. The research also found that Belfast has little experience of segregation returning to previous levels after a violent episode ends. The research concludes that, while segregation falls during quiet times, it does not fall back to preceding levels and therefore the overall trend is inexorably upward. Catholics were found to occupy a limited area in Belfast West, are more likely to be living in areas where they are the minority, and are more likely to be living in mixed areas. Combined, these findings have led to an overall increase in residential segregation within the Urban Area. The highest level of segregation is in Belfast West, while the lowest levels are found in the more middle-class areas of Belfast South and Holywood. Finally, the method of segregation has remained the same: members of the minority in an area are intimidated from their homes, or leave voluntarily because of insecurities.

24. East Belfast Community Development Agency (2001) *Leading from Behind: An Agenda for Change* in East Belfast. Belfast, EBCDA.

'Leading from Behind' provides comprehensive, up-to-date information about the local communities of East Belfast. This report provides in-depth demographic and deprivation information for the fourteen East Belfast neighbourhoods, and identifies extreme patterns of inequality in the area. The research evaluates educational qualifications and employment rates for the local area, as well as overall satisfaction with the local area. A lacklustre attitude towards community activities is recorded. This report identifies a lack of health information and under-utilization of community and youth facilities. The community intends to utilise these findings by developing a strategy that addresses local needs and concerns.

25. Ellis, Geraint and McKay, Stephen (2000) City Management Profile Belfast. *Cities*, Vol. 17, No. 1.

This study examines the geographical and institutional framework of Belfast and discusses the city's future in light of the peace process. The study begins by providing a synopsis of the ethnic tensions, economic decline and high unemployment rates, which hinder economic growth in Belfast. Population changes and the recent phenomenon of urban decentralisation are mostly attributed to violent political conflict, while encouraged migration and the availability of private housing have also influenced relocation decisions.

The research found that the institutional and political structures of Northern Ireland are derived from the turbulent political history. Direct Rule, the lack of direct representation and the 'democratic deficit' are discussed and it is claimed that reforms were hindered as they required unattainable political consensus. The research discusses the two ways in which Belfast City Council influences the future development of Belfast, namely the sustainable development strategy and the Development Committee. The research goes on to delineate the shared power and responsibility of the Northern Ireland Secretary of State, the Department of the Environment and the six Planning Services regarding developing and implementing planning strategies. The unique role of the Northern Ireland Housing Executive and subsequent role upon urban management is discussed.

The strategy for the urban regeneration of Belfast was specially created to meet the specific problems of Northern Ireland. This planning strategy was found to be based upon partnerships, community infrastructure and access to EU finances. The research includes case-studies of regeneration from the Laganside regeneration, Springfield Initiative and Making Belfast Work. The successes of these programmes remain linked to the management of conflict and economic decline in the city.

The study goes on to analyse the new forms of governance in Northern Ireland. The Assembly and Executive are found to facilitate locally accountable decisions on urban management issues. It is established that a more stable economic climate would facilitate investment and business integration. The research concludes that a new civil society is emerging in Belfast and must address lingering problems. The study remains optimistic for the economic future of Northern Ireland.

26. Fay, Marie Therese; Morrissey, Mike; Smyth, Marie and Wong, Tracy (1999) *The Cost of the Troubles Study.* **Derry, INCORE/Cost of the Troubles Study.**

The Cost of the Troubles Study explores the range of Troubles–related occurrences experienced by Northern Ireland citizens and analyses the subsequent physical and psychological effects. The research reports significant trends between areas with high intensity, medium intensity and low intensity numbers of politically motivated deaths. In summary, high intensity wards reported low educational attainment, high levels of unemployment, high levels of benefit dependency and a majority Catholic population. The medium intensity wards reported an increase in home ownership, marital status, educational qualification and an increasing Protestant population. The trends in low intensity wards included a larger population of elderly residents, low unemployment, low numbers of single parents and a Protestant majority.

The report analyses location, gender, age and socio-economic status as variables for Troubles-related experiences. Regarding location, low-income households and high benefit dependency characterised high intensity areas. Individuals in high-intensity wards felt more strongly that their lives had been altered by the Troubles. The study found sharp and significant differences between the religions, with Catholics more likely to be affected by the violence. Age was established as a key variable in relation to exposure of violence. Contrary to previous research, the 25-39 year-old groups reported the most experience of the Troubles.

The study applies a standard health measure to all respondents and finds that individuals from high-intensity areas reported the lowest scores on all scales. The research measures those who suffer symptoms of Post-Traumatic Stress Disorder by religion, age and location. The sub-group, which reported severe and very severe experiences of the Troubles, was further analysed. The report concludes by offering recommendations to multiple service providers. It calls for recognition of cost factors in developing and delivering compensatory policies. The need for spatially targeted programmes for individual areas is recommended.

27. Forthspring Inter-Community Group and Belfast Exposed (2001) *The Hurt, the Peace, the Love and the War.* **Belfast, Forthspring Inter-Community Group.**

This photo journal contains many striking images of daily life along both sides of the Springfield Road - Woodvale peace line. Poetry and captions accompany the black and white images, and address topics of peace, identity and loss.

28. Gaffikin, Frank; Morrissey, Michael and Sterrett, Ken (2001) Remaking the City: the Role of Culture in Belfast. In William Neill and Hanns-Uve Schwedler (eds) *Urban Planning and Cultural Inclusion: Lessons from Belfast and Berlin.* **Basingstoke, Palgrave.**

This article examines the contribution of culture towards Belfast urban regeneration. The researchers identify a sequence of planning initiatives proposed to re-shape the city in the post-industrial era. The publication considers the economic potential of cultural industries in the city, especially regarding deprived communities. Belfast's capacity to successfully emphasise cultural industries is considered, along with the impact of urban regeneration on social division. The research argues that Belfast remains an important regional centre and would benefit from restoration schemes, which would promote service and knowledge based economic development.

Section Two: *Belfast at the Crossroads; the Need for a Multicultural City* identifies two sets of crossroads confronting city planners: economic issues and social and political division. The research identifies Belfast as a divided city with split ethnic territories and contested spaces and the need to highlight the benefits of a multicultural city. The article recommends a post-industrial future, where rival cultures can find synergy, rather than conflict, in their differences.

Section Three: *Economic and Physical Modernization in Belfast* recognises that state intervention has been unable to achieve necessary economic modernisation. The section examines the 1969 Belfast Urban Plan, which emphasised redevelopment, industrial growth and suburban lifestyles, but coincided with the political crisis and led to plummeting investments and abandoned developments.

Section Four: *Post-Industrial Belfast* examines 1980s Urban Planning. The research identifies a shift towards services, focusing on developing the central business district and Lagan waterfront, which aimed to assist regeneration and attract investments for the city.

Section Five: *Boosting Belfast in the 1990s* discusses the events intended to boost Belfast's international reputation and shows how the city centre regeneration was dependent upon addressing and amending deep social divisions.

Section Six: *Social and Sectarian Divisions* traces the population movement between 1971-1991 and emphasises the problem of deepening segregation across the city. It examines the revival of the city centre, and concludes that these investments benefited commuters rather than residents. The section discusses economic deprivation in North and West Belfast and argues that the urban poor have remained spatially contained in enclosures that inhibit physical and economic access to city opportunities.

Section Seven: *A Tale of Two Cities: Downtown vs. Neighbourhoods* examines the UK-wide trend for urban revitalisation which tends to produce highly segmented and economically divided cities, as development is more concerned with profit and image than social need and ecology. However, the study notes the importance of supporting economic growth and political recovery. The research shows that Belfast's deprived communities did not receive a proportional share of benefit from previous regeneration schemes and emphasises the profitability of a well-developed cultural sector.

Section Eight: *The Role of Arts and Culture in Belfast Regeneration* examines the role of cultural industries in revitalisation and restoration projects and lists the accomplishments and difficulties of this proposal. This section examines the difference in support between traditional arts and local community arts in Belfast, and suggests a Community Arts Corridor linking North and West Belfast to the City Centre.

Section Nine: *Cultural Industries: The Problem of Definition* examines the relationship between economic development and the changing composition of demand.

Section Ten: *Culture and the Economy: Key Dimensions* identifies six distinct dimensions of the relationship between culture and the economy. The research emphasises the need to go beyond economic dimensions to recognise the social wealth created through the arts. This section concludes by examining how cultural expression operates in conflicted areas, and the importance of neutral space. Finally the authors propose the creation of genuinely 'shared space' alongside 'ethnic' 'neutral' and 'transcendence' space, to express a common belonging to the city.

29. **Gallagher, Ryan (ed) (2000)** *BT5: A Photographic Exploration of Identity by Young People in East Belfast.* **Belfast, Wheelworks.**

This publication examines the attitudes and perceptions of young people from Catholic/Nationalist Short Strand and Protestant/Unionist Inner

East Belfast through the medium of photography. The participants identify positive and negative features of their local area, along with daily sights and places.

30. **Garvaghy Residents (1999)** *Garvaghy: A Community Under Siege.* **Belfast, Beyond the Pale Publications.**

Garvaghy: A Community Under Siege provides a Nationalist perspective on Orange Order marches on the Garvaghy Road. The first half of this publication provides personal accounts from fourteen Garvaghy Road residents during the 1998 marching season. Many similar themes were found in these individual observations, including fear of attack, unity between community members, lack of trust in security forces, a siege mentality, increased tensions and the effects of sectarian murders upon the entire community. Notably, the residents indicated more concern towards parade hangers-on, rather than Orange Order marchers.

The second section of the book traces the contentious and violent history associated with Orange marches in Portadown and traces the history of parading in the local area from 1795 until 1999. It argues that the area has endured devastating sectarian violence due to violent and illegal parades. Due to the cyclical nature of the parading season, similar problems were encountered every year without satisfactory solutions or initiatives. The section also includes an abridged version of Looking into the Abyss: Report from the Garvaghy Road Portadown July 4-6 1997, complied by PeaceWatch Ireland. This publication concludes that the Orange Order has forfeited its right to walk Garvaghy Road because of its refusal to meet community representatives. Any attempts toward future compromises have been severely hindered because of ongoing violence.

31. **Hall, Michael (ed) (2005)** *Finding Common Ground: An Exploration by Young People from both Sides of the East Belfast Interface.* **Newtownabbey, Island Publications.**

Finding Common Ground examines attempts to build bridges after the 2002 violence between Inner East Belfast communities, through a discussion led by a cross-community group of young people exploring community safety, education and cross-community interaction. The discussion details the lack of facilities available to young people. The group agreed that the anti-social behaviour of a few individuals tarnishes the reputation of young people in their community. The group also discussed the residual tensions between two areas, and agreed that restrictions were slowly lifting and a sense of normality was returning to the area. An ongoing criminality/thug element was found to be present in the area, and the young people expressed a sense of powerlessness about this reality. The need for an acceptable police force was emphasised. The group put forward several interventionist-type strategies to address the low-level criminality.

The young people described the riots as exciting and an adrenaline rush, and could report no comparable satisfaction in community-based programmes. Participation in the riots fulfilled a dual function of recreational activity and defending one's community. The adult reaction to youth participation in riots was mixed, and caused confusion within the participants. The riots left a harmful legacy upon the area, and the young people concurred that they would not return to rioting for recreational purposes.

The perceptions and benefits of cross-community work are also analysed, with many respondents reporting that meeting individuals successfully challenged group labels. Common concerns were found between the communities, as the young people discussed the lack of local facilities, the importance of religion in their daily life, and the harmful effect of anti-social behaviour upon their communities. The group concurred that community restrictions were slowly lifting, but residual tensions continued. The young people reported a sense of powerlessness about their community, and reported concerns about policing and ongoing anti-social behaviour. The attraction of young people to violent situations, along with the distrustful relationship between young people and paramilitaries are commented upon. The study calls for further research, more community provision and community-led intervention and the importance of engaging with young people in creating meaningful dialogue is emphasised.

32. **Hall, Michael (ed) (2004)** *Exploring the Marching Issue: Views from Nationalist North Belfast.* **Newtownabbey, Island Publications.**

This pamphlet examines attitudes of Nationalists in North Belfast towards the onset of the annual summer marching season. Although most parades are trouble-free, several have sparked inter-community bloodshed and interface violence. While the Parades Commission has the authority to decide whether or not a parade can proceed, and allocate necessary restrictions, few people in either community are satisfied with the current situation. The pamphlet describes community members' frustrations towards the marching season. Several group members discussed feeling intimidated during parades, due to sectarian chants and references to paramilitary groups. Community workers explained that parades harmed cross-community work and increased interface tensions. The group felt that there were contradictions in attempting to contest Orange marches along with working to establish meaningful links with the Protestant community. The discussions also revealed the difficulties within the Nationalist community in finding a community-wide consensus towards parades. The group maintained two differing opinions: either Nationalists remain firmly opposed to any parading routes, or Nationalists accept parading rights once parade organisers accept and acknowledge the rights of their community.

The group struggled to establish consistent reasons for community opposition to Orange parades. While some members were only against Orange regalia, flags and paramilitary trappings, others remained inherently opposed to any Orange presence within their community. This led to discussion over how the Nationalist community could conduct productive talks with the Loyal Orders if minority groups remained inherently opposed to the organisation. Although the majority wanted to engage in talks with the Loyal Orders, the group could not reach a consensus about possible negotiation points, concessions, or an overall objective.

33. Hall, Michael (ed) (2003) *Beginning a Debate: An Exploration by Ardoyne Community Activists.* Newtownabbey, Island Publications.

This study presents an analysis of ongoing sectarian tension and interface violence across North Belfast, especially in relation to the Holy Cross dispute. The research is a record of ten Ardoyne community leaders discussing rising sectarian attitudes as a result of the Holy Cross dispute. The participants discussed the fall-out of the Holy Cross conflict upon their community. Many acknowledged that the protest was a symptom of larger problems between the two communities. Several members described the interface as unfixable, and stated how many community residents preferred to ignore the problem.

Many participants agreed that people needed to reinforce their own culture and identity before constructively engaging with outsiders. This conversation illustrated the lingering divisions within the community, most notably between those who wanted to call on Republicans to resolve Holy Cross, and those who preferred local dialogue and discussion within the community. This split exemplifies the different stances within the community regarding effective problem-solving methods. The discussion addressed the perceived bias of media presentation during the Holy Cross dispute. One community worker argued that misrepresentation harmed cross-community relations, and thus provided another excuse to raise tensions.

The group mentioned the positive changes taking place in the Ardoyne. Although acknowledging the direness of Holy Cross, one member noted how this harmful situation had encouraged different community members to unify for a common goal. Another member acknowledged how the Church was actively encouraging and improving intra-community relations. Regarding the ongoing interface problems, members maintained a variety of perceptions about the situation and potential solutions. One member was hesitant to continue cross-community dialogue at that time, believing neither side was ready to engage with the other. Some group members discussed disappointing results from previous cross-community work, noting that groups did not confront the hard issues. Another common concern was the existing apathy within community members to accept, rather than confront, difficult issues.

The dialogue concluded with participants suggesting different ways to confront sectarianism. Members voiced many diverse ideas, such as stronger anti-sectarian legislation, breaking the generational cycle, and confronting class inequality. The group felt that despite the problems surrounding Holy Cross, the Ardoyne community was taking positive steps towards the future.

34. Hall, Michael (ed) (2003) *The East Belfast Interface (1): Lower Newtownards Youth Speak Out*. Newtownabbey, Island Publications.

This publication is a compilation of viewpoints from the Lower Newtownards Road, a Protestant area bordering Short Strand. The relationship between the Catholic area of Short Strand and surrounding Protestant East Belfast had been strained, but had remained free from large-scale sectarian violence within recent years until May 2002, when inter-communal violence erupted. Both Protestant and Catholic communities blamed the other side for starting and continuing the violence. This pamphlet incorporates the viewpoint and experiences of four youth and community workers and seven young people from the Lower Newtownards Road.

The first half of the report contains comments and opinions from Lower Newtownards Road youth workers. The group agreed that the absence of adequate youth provisions in the area harmed community development.

The youth workers also discussed their previous experience of applying for funding through statutory agencies, and their shared beliefs that funding agencies did not understand the needs of interface communities. The group were also frustrated by the lack of long-term funding, as this hindered their ability to plan certain activities. However, the youth workers remained optimistic that single-identity programmes would challenge sectarian attitudes on the Lower Newtownards Road.

The second half of the pamphlet is a recorded discussion between young males of the Lower Newtownards community. The main themes of this conversation were interface violence, problems at school and future goals. The group identified the twin issues of boredom and inability to travel outside the area as the biggest hardships facing their community. The young people recalled experiences of being denied entry into local leisure facilities, and feeling relegated to hanging around on street corners. Problems in school were also discussed, as many group members felt unfairly branded as "troublemakers" by school officials. These young people identified that gambling at their local arcade, rather than illegal drug use or underage drinking, was the greatest problem in their area. The group concluded by acknowledging how interface rioting defaced their community and set a goal of projecting a positive image for East Belfast.

35. Hall, Michael (ed) (2003) *The East Belfast Interface (2): Short Strand Youth Speak Out.* **Newtownabbey, Island Publications.**

This is a compilation of viewpoints from the Short Strand area of east Belfast. The pamphlet incorporates the views of five youth and community workers, and eight young people living in Short Strand. The first half of the pamphlet is devoted to the comments and viewpoint of the youth and community workers. The Short Strand has approximately 2,500 residents, with a large percentage of young people and high unemployment rates. Although Short Strand previously maintained an active cross-community programme, the recent violence has halted this project. The workers indicated that outside people did not understand the enormity of conducting cross-community work in East Belfast. As a result of interface trouble, the workers reported many negative changes to the Short Strand community. Most apparent were the increase in anti-social behaviour, a further loss of confidence in the PSNI and overworked community volunteers. The Short Strand workers constantly re-iterated how they felt responsible for holding their community together during the summer, but lacked adequate resources for this task. Although many high-end businesses have opened in nearby areas, local residents cannot acquire the qualifications necessary for employment.

Finally, the workers stated their willingness to re-establish links with nearby Protestant communities, but expressed frustration regarding paramilitary approval of their programmes.

The second half of this work illustrates the experiences of young people living in Short Strand. The lack of accessible leisure facilities was the biggest concern raised by the young people, which reinforced the earlier statements made by community workers. The young people agreed that drug use is a substantial problem in their area, and predicted that the drug culture will continue to grow. Another topic discussed by the young people was difficulty travelling to different areas. The group recounted events, such as the bricking of school buses and sectarian graffiti, which left them apprehensive about venturing outside Short Strand. When asked to describe the long-term effects of interface rioting, young people reported feeling scared to walk local streets, and being unable to access the post office or chemist. Additionally, the young people felt stigmatised for living in the Short Strand, and recounted difficulties getting jobs or mobile phone contracts because of their address. Finally, the group expressed frustration about the overall grubbiness of their community, but concluded that cleaning was a waste, as everything would only be wrecked in the next riot.

36. Hall, Michael (ed) (2003) *It's Good to Talk: The Experiences of the Springfield Mobile Phone Network.* Newtownabbey, Island Publications.

This study reviews the history and experiences of the Springfield mobile phone network. The legacy of suspicion and misunderstanding between the communities at this West Belfast interface has existed through the duration of the Troubles, and has caused extensive damage to both sides of the community. The summer of 1996 was a particularly difficult time, as fear, rumours and misunderstandings across the interface led to substantial violence. Community activists from both sides endeavoured to find an adequate response to this crisis and, with assistance from the Community Development Centre, established a mobile phone network to promote dialogue and dispel rumours around the interface area. Six years on, the members of the Springfield Inter-Community Forum continue to participate in the phone network.

The pamphlet describes discussions between the Springfield mobile phone holders, in relation to the successes and shortcoming of the programme. The group felt that the programme offered a practical means of responding to outbreaks of youth-inspired interface violence, and often prevented minor incidents from developing into serious situations. The participants also agreed that violent incidents across the interface had substantially decreased since the mobile phone network began operating. However, group members recalled the numerous difficulties faced by their network, such as suspicions voiced within their own community, and the personal stress of participating in an unpaid, time-consuming project. One group member also stated that while the mobile phone network was able to address youth violence, phone holders were unable to quell orchestrated paramilitary violence.

The group described their relationship with the police, and these opinions remained divided along community lines. The Unionist representatives, unlike their Nationalist counterparts, felt that contact with the police in the run-up to summer marches was vital for event safety. While some spoke about their positive interactions with local police, others voiced distrust about many PSNI practices. The participants also discussed the influence of Northern Ireland-wide tensions upon local interface violence. Many group members expressed an opinion that West Belfast was easier to monitor than North Belfast, as community activists only monitored one interface; they expressed relief that their area had not experienced a 'Holy Cross' style crisis.

The group also discussed the subject of young people. Participants agreed that youths were deeply affected by the high levels of social deprivation. Participants further concurred that young people were the greatest cause of interface trouble, and identified bonfires as magnets for anti-social elements. In order to combat these problems, members discussed the need for a long-term youth strategy. In conclusion, participants agreed that the Springfield Inter-Community Forum mobile phone network had reduced tensions and violence in both communities. Despite the constant struggle for funding and unpredictable political events, the mobile phone network had created unprecedented cross-community involvement. Although community relations remained a complex problem, the Springfield mobile phone group had successfully defused volatile interface situations and decreased interface tensions.

37. Hall, Michael (ed) (2002) *Reuniting the Shankill: A Report on the Greater Shankill Community Exhibition and Convention.* **Newtownabbey, Island Publications.**

This pamphlet is a recorded account of community dialogue compiled after the 2001 Loyalist feud. The Shankill community was deeply affected by bitter Loyalist in-fighting, seven people were killed during the hostilities, and hundreds more fled their homes. In response to this inter-community conflict, the Church of Ireland helped form the Loyalist Commission, with representatives from different churches, political parties, community groups and paramilitary organisations, in order to prevent another outbreak of violence. The Commission aspired to heal community divisions, restore confidence among local residents and build a positive future agenda. One product of the Loyalist Commission was the Greater Shankill Community Exhibition and Convention, which provided a forum for different community groups and local residents to come together and discuss community issues.

The first section of the pamphlet contains the minutes of the meeting of the Greater Shankill Community Convention. Twelve broad issues were raised by participants, including housing concerns, youth provision, jobs and employment, information and funding support, drug and alcohol abuse, counselling, local networking, the Shankill as an arterial route, the needs of interface areas, anti-social behaviour, parading, policing and human rights. Each of these subjects then became an open workshop.

The author records the workshops on Anti-Social Behaviour and Policing. The Anti-Social Behaviour workshop opened with most participants agreeing that anti-social behaviour posed a large problem to the Shankill community. The inability of young people and adults to engage constructively with each other was identified as a significant problem, and the adult participants hoped to bridge this gap by involving young people in future community forums. Several adults were also critical of local churches, believing these institutions to have re-directed their focus away from young people. The group questioned the role of local paramilitaries in contributing to anti-social behaviour, and agreed these organisations should carry some responsibility for the high levels of community disorder.

The Policing and Human Rights workshop discussed a range of community concerns. The forum was convinced that local police were biased against their community, and deliberately incorporated heavy-handed tactics. Participants also discussed the current education system, with some participants reporting that it failed to meet the needs of local students. Finally, several residents reported prejudicial stereotyping from police and prospective employers for having a BT13 postcode. Both leaders and audience were overwhelmingly positive about the event. The group discussed ways of involving more community members, and decided to bring summary information to the attention of the Loyalist Commission and encourage participants to remain enthusiastic about this project for the long-term future.

38. Hall, Michael (ed) (2002) *An Uncertain Future: An Exploration by Protestant Community Activists.* Newtownabbey, Island Publications.

This Think Tank Project is a series of discussions between eleven Protestant community workers from across Belfast. Initially, the community workers began by describing the daily challenges within Protestant working-class communities and identified high unemployment, low educational attainment, weak community infrastructure, and a lack of long-term strategies for revitalisation and renewal as major community problems.

The group began by discussing the negative perception of local politicians within their community. The majority of participants felt that local politicians did not understand local problems and made no effort to locate community funding. The group believed that Unionist politicians were far behind their Nationalist counterparts in terms of 'on the ground' political participation and attempts to secure funding for community interests. The community workers also addressed the deep political divisions within the Protestant community. One respondent stated that community workers helped to bring people together, while politicians and political parties created new community divisions. The group held a bleak outlook for the future of their communities, and agreed that the Protestant community was lacking strong leadership and were constantly dividing and isolating themselves.

A further discussion point was the Holy Cross dispute. The group perceived that the Glenbryn protest had started without coherent objectives and the situation was dragging itself out. The participants explained that local protestors were not fixated on attacking Catholic schoolchildren, but in showing their anger to the government. Many participants agreed that the media had misinterpreted the situation. One community worker felt that Glenbryn residents had reasons to protest, but were relying on self-defeating methods.

Finally, the community workers discussed the poor relationship with funders. The group agreed that funders' goals were sometimes impractical, as their goals and practical community goals are often very different. The pamphlet concludes with a discussion on future community strategies. Many participants agreed that the Protestant community were caught up in small-scale projects, and should instead be focusing on long-term objectives. Many also hoped that leading Unionist politicians would become more involved in local community activities.

The group concluded that local community work had brought positive benefits to many local areas, but many issues remained unresolved.

39. Hall, Michael (ed) (2001) *Community Relations: An Elusive Concept.* **Newtownabbey, Island Publications.**

This study begins by outlining sectarian tensions and high deprivation levels within working-class communities across North Belfast. Neighbouring Protestant and Catholic communities share a confusing and changing patchwork of interfaces, where the ongoing violence has re-affirmed deep-seated fears of the 'other' community. Over the years, community workers have struggled to deal with multiple problems within the area, but the strong sectarian division has hindered many attempts at 'community relations'. This report incorporates the views of ten North Belfast community activists.

Group members discussed the constant misconceptions of CR work by local residents. The community activists also discussed how local residents remained inherently suspicious of community relations' work. The group agreed that a defined goal and clear definitions of community relations would increase community support. The preference of community workers was to focus on community development rather than cross-community work. Numerous participants agreed that many more important needs currently existed within their communities rather than the state of Protestant/Catholic relations. Some activists expressed their frustration at government and funding policy, which they felt were focused on community relations, rather than social class issues.

The group argued that sectarian attitudes were perpetuated by government agencies and civil servants. The community leaders voiced concerns that particular people created policies for interface areas without truly understanding the situation. The community activists agreed that problems in North Belfast resulted from a cycle of deprivation, alienation and violence. However, residents from both communities remained unwilling to discuss contentious issues in mixed company. This perpetuated a cycle of resentment and unresolved complaints. They provided examples of cross-community work that occurred without government funding. Participants agreed that long-term progress involved improving relations across the sectarian divide, but local residents could not be forced to engage in certain activities.

Unrealistic cross-community goals maintained by funders was discussed. The activists felt funders held unrealistic expectations about progress in

North Belfast and encouraged community groups to aggressively compete for limited resources. Finally they listed the difficulties in defining community relations. The group agreed that community relations work should not be separated from community development work and acknowledged that many communities were dealing with a crisis level in community relations. The community activists anticipated focusing on their cross-community accomplishments, while avoiding burdening themselves or their community with unrealistic expectations.

40. Hall, Michael (ed) (2001) *Young People Speak Out: Newhill Youth Development Team.* **Newtownabbey, Island Publications.**

This study examines the attitudes and perceptions of young people from a Nationalist working-class community in West Belfast. The participants were members of the Newhill Youth Development Team. This team gives young people a sense of ownership and responsibility within their area and a forum for discussing relevant issues. Ten young people contributed their views on politics, religion and cross-community relations for this pamphlet.

The first section *Part of the Community* discusses the perceptions of young people within their community. Group members felt that adults within their community made no effort to understand young people's concerns, and stigmatised all young people as 'anti-social'. The second section *Sense of Belonging* addressed the ties between young people and their community. Most group members were enthusiastic about their future employment prospects, but emphasised their decision to eventually return and settle in their community. The third section *School - A Failed Promise* contained a catalogue of concerns regarding the local education system. The young people disliked their school environment and believed the education system failed to prepare students for real-world difficulties.

The fourth section *Living with the Troubles* details the daily lives of young people before the Good Friday Agreement. The group members were quick to point out the numerous ways in which the Troubles affected their entire community. The group saw nothing unusual in rioting and attacking the security forces, indicating that these activities were part of a normal society. Several group members described the element of excitement in their almost ritualised confrontations with the security forces.

The fifth section *Cross-Community Activities* describes the young people's previous experiences of interacting with their Protestant counterparts.

While some group members had positive cross-community experiences, and others encountered outright hostility, the entire group agreed on the merits of cross-community contact. The group also agreed that outsiders had the most trouble understanding Belfast issues.

The sixth section *Religion* illustrates how young people incorporated their identity based on their community background, rather than actual church attendance.

The seventh section *War and Peace* documents the group's uncertainty about the Good Friday Agreement. While every group member was encouraged by the promises of the GFA, many were uncertain that paramilitary violence had permanently ended. When discussing the legacy of the IRA, group members indicated an understanding of IRA actions, but there was no cohesive agreement about paramilitary procedures.

The eighth section *Political Awareness* discusses the frustration young people felt with Northern Irish politics. The group agreed that most young people were uneducated about important political decisions. Political education and single-identity work were viewed as likely to motivate more residents to contribute to local politics.

The ninth section *Pressures of Everyday Life* addresses a number of social concerns. Group members were very concerned about suicide, teenage pregnancy and drug use, all of which negatively affected their friends and their community. The group believed that the government had overlooked these issues during the worst of the 'Troubles' and now needed to address these problems. The young people discussed unemployment and lack of community participation by young people and agreed that there were few opportunities for young people within their area.

41. Hall, Michael (ed) (1999) *Living in a Mixed Community: The Experiences of Ballynafeigh*. Newtownabbey, Island Publications.

The Ballynafeigh community, located on Belfast's Ormeau Road, has historically been a community of mixed religion, social class and ethnicity. The success of this community has inspired several like-minded projects. This pamphlet examines how the community has confronted problems such as anti-social behaviour, bonfires, and community development. The pamphlet records discussions between fifteen Ballynafeigh residents.

Many group members recalled being attracted to the idea of living in a mixed community. However, the group was quick to point out that their community was not fully mixed, and that small enclaves and invisible interfaces existed. Another resident recalled past problems of sectarian intimidation, specifically during the marching season. Residents agreed that their community experienced increased anticipation and fear during the marching season, similar to the rest of Belfast. The media problem was also discussed, with residents agreeing that the media were quick to report trouble, but slow in reporting positive change. Several residents voiced concerns about outsiders travelling to Ballynafeigh, intent on causing trouble and raising tensions. The group concluded by discussing their displeasure about year-long marching season decorations.

The District Master of Ballynafeigh Orange Lodge discussed his efforts to prevent retaliatory violence, and his disappointment over certain communities succumbing to paramilitary influence. Several residents voiced their frustration with Nationalist leadership, and their seeming inability to compromise on parading issues. The final section addresses the needs of young people in the Ballynafeigh community. Despite living in this mixed community, these young people recounted incidents of sectarian intimidation and harassment. Additionally, these participants felt that Ballynafeigh lacked youth facilities, and they also relayed their unwillingness to use nearby Church-based organisations. There was also an acknowledgement from the young people about the growing drug culture in their community.

The pamphlet concludes with residents discussing how to improve the community. Many spoke of wanting to restore their area and re-establish a sense of neighbourliness. Notably, the points raised on this topic were primarily antisocial behaviour issues, rather than sectarian problems. The group generated many positive ideas for Ballynafeigh, including applying for funding, addressing the invisible boundaries and participating in cross-community events. The discussion ended on a note of cautious optimism, with residents reminded to be realistic in their aspirations about changing their community.

42. Hamilton, Michael (2001) *Working Relationships: An Evaluation of Community Mobile Phone Networks in Northern Ireland*. Belfast, Community Relations Council.

This report presents important findings on existing Mobile Phone Networks (MPN's), which link community volunteers in neighbouring areas through the provision of mobile phones, thereby improving communication within and between communities and between communities and statutory agencies. The report provides a comprehensive assessment of the contributions that MPN's have made towards reducing community tensions.

The research traces the history of MPN's. It is argued that MPN's benefit local communities, young people, the police, the Housing Executive, the Department of the Environment and District Councils. Phone holders provide a variety of services for individual communities, including addressing interface rumours, contacting statutory agencies and liasing with police. The report found that MPN's are most effective at quashing rumours and de-escalating violent situations, and least effective in dealing with paramilitary-orchestrated situations. The most crucial factor to the operation of a successful MPN is an agreement of mutual responsibility between individual phone holders.

Several difficulties related to MPN's were identified. Notably, the responsibility for funding and the fact that sustaining MPN's does not lie with any specific statutory agency. Subsequently, funding has been erratic and inconsistent for certain networks. The ability to locate an appropriate community activist willing to hold a phone also affects the success of MPN's. Finally, MPN's require substantial trust between cross-community phone holders, and phone holders are continually combating problems of community mistrust.

The report includes case studies on specific MPN's in the Springfield Inter Community Development Group, the Inner East Interface Project, Derry Londonderry, Portadown, Carrickfergus, Antrim and other Belfast networks. The report is unable to place a price on the damage, riots and destruction averted, but credits the MPN's with greatly limiting the human and political costs of violence.

The report makes several recommendations to increase MPN productivity, including the production of official guidelines for all phone holders, and defining relationships between phone holders, the police and statutory agencies. The report also discusses formal training and increased recognition for all phone holders, and concludes with a list of potential funding bodies.

43. Heatley, Colm (2004) *Interface: Flashpoints in Northern Ireland.* **Belfast, Lagan Books Publishing**

This book examines the circumstances behind violence between interface communities. It examines the specific circumstances of numerous areas in North and West Belfast, Short Strand, Derry Londonderry, Garvaghy Road, Dunloy and Bellaghy. The study examines a variety of interface areas in Belfast, Derry Londonderry and rural areas and finds overlapping problems and concerns.

Territoriality, or the use and availability of land, is identified as a severe source of inter-community conflict. Fears regarding territoriality have sparked concerns over available housing, accusations of ethnic cleansing and worries over demographic change and subsequent encroachment. Parading concerns have also consistently divided interface communities as Parade Commission decisions, policing difficulties and parade violence have sparked sustained interface rioting throughout the marching season. The research discusses the dynamics of community cohesion, where a single parade decision has caused violent protests, blockades and shows of unity throughout Northern Ireland. The existing fear and mistrust between communities is identified as a major obstacle that hinders cross-community dialogue and mediation, while the role of paramilitaries within violent situations is discussed and analysed.

The research presents many opposing political viewpoints on a number of interface concerns. The author stresses the importance of politicians serving their entire constituency, rather than specific religious communities. The multiple deprivations suffered by interface communities are discussed, along with concerns over the role of young people in sustaining interface violence. The research concludes by reassessing political, cultural and interface concerns, and presents viable suggestions for future politicians of Northern Ireland.

44. Henry, Pat; Hawthorne, Isy; McCready, Sam and Campbell, Hugh (2002) *The Summer of 2002: An evaluation of the impact of diversionary funding for work with young people in Belfast interfaces during the summer of 2002.* Belfast, Belfast Education and Library Board.

This report analyses the impact of diversionary activities in reducing interface violence and the role of funding in establishing sustainable development. The research employed numerous methods of data collection across a number of summer schemes that received additional diversionary funding. The impact of parades, policing, territoriality, segregation, violence and deprivation upon local communities is analysed. The issues that impede planning, such as uncertain financial support, reliance upon volunteers and lack of inter-agency communication are discussed. The report proposes measures to better administer available summer-scheme provisions.

The research contains a comprehensive literature review regarding interface activities and antisocial behaviour. Diversionary activities have been found to limit both sectarian violence and 'normal' anti-social behaviour. The potential of programmes that combat crime in Scotland, England and Wales to provide new ideas for Belfast programmes is discussed. The report advocates that diversionary activities should be set within the policy context of Northern Ireland.

The study concludes that diversionary funding has a significant impact on young people from interface areas, and advocates substantial resources for lengthy programmes. The report stresses the importance of engaging with older age groups, which typically requires expensive diversionary activities. The timing of additional funding was found to be crucial to the availability and publicity of programmes.

45. Hepburn, A.C.H. (1994) Long Divisions and Ethnic Conflict: The Experiences of Belfast. In Seamus Dunn (ed) *Managing Divided Cities.* Keele, Ryburn Publishing.

This chapter examines ethnic rioting in Belfast from 1813 until the present day, and measures the influence of labour, housing and politics in perpetuating sectarian divisions. It argues that most cities are ethnically mixed, and that when consciousness of existing differences is sufficiently persuasive, numerous problems, including cultural division of labour, housing and access to resources, occur. The population shifts of majority and minority groups are identified as directly affecting the housing market, voting patterns and the political balance within a region. The chapter maintains that cities exist as visible cockpits of ethnic struggle, with the capacity to influence the context in which ethnic settlements are made and questions whether urban ethnic division can ever be settled internally, or if state action or enforced population movement are always required.

Hepburn identifies three significant changes in Belfast demographics since the 18th century. First the rapid economic growth based on factory production of textiles, which encouraged Catholic workers to settle in Belfast. The second phase, between 1861-1911, recorded an increase in Protestant numbers with a correlating decrease in Catholic migrants. The third demographic change followed the end of the Second World War, as the Catholic population steadily increased. The author argues that the most important demographic phase in Belfast's history was the Protestant surge between 1861-1911, which ensured that Belfast remained Protestant politically and in all-important areas of the economy and labour market. The author asserts that the existence of Protestant Belfast maintained the image of Protestant Ulster and effectively intimidated the British government into developing the partition policy between 1912-1920. The section concludes that recent demographic trends are unlikely to instigate significant political change.

Hepburn details the prevalence of residential and territorial segregation in Belfast since the mid-seventeenth century and identifies four main phases of development in this pattern. Between the late 18th century and mid-19th century, a significant number of Catholic enclaves were created within the Protestant city. The second phase, after the 1845-46 Famine, established Belfast's characteristic segregated residential pattern, was marked by continuous long-term rioting and was characterised by tight encirclement of most Catholic enclaves. The period from 1935-1968, the longest period in Belfast history without riotous confrontation, constitutes a third phase. However, this phase saw little easing of segregated residential patterns. In the fourth phase, since the mid-1960s, segregation reached higher levels than ever before, due to chronic violence and disorder. He then analyses the contributions of public sector housing to the situation, and concludes that Housing Executive policies have encouraged segregation by prioritising victims of intimidation and responding to pressures for security through separation.

The study concludes by addressing the conflicting ethnic trends in contemporary Belfast society. While there are more mixed marriages and middle-class workers, there has been no reduction in residential or workplace segregation. The researcher maintains that an effective equal opportunities programme would address this situation and reduce the likelihood for serious ethnic violence. According to the research, the Ulster conflict is unique because neither side has the strength to drive out the other unaided, nor is there likelihood of intervention by third parties. The chapter concludes that ethnic separation has been an underlying trend over a very long period, and not a simple knee-jerk response to recent troubles.

46. Inter-Action Belfast (2004) *Strategic Plan 2004-2007.* **Belfast, Inter-Action Belfast.**

This publication outlines the seven key objectives of Inter-action Belfast for 2004-2007. The operational goals for the establishment include improving quality of life for interface communities and sustaining and building cross-community relations across community institutions. The publication contends that peace building should not focus strictly on successful conflict resolution, but improving the quality of life for marginalised residents and communities. The main aims of Inter-Action are identified as:

1. **Resolving Differences** through utilising models of best practice from previous work. They aim to address concerns over two key areas, cross community dialogue and graffiti, flags and emblems.
2. **Community Development Across the Interface** emphasises the community development core of operational practice. The study identifies a strong correlation between poverty and interface communities, and aims to work towards developing shared prosperity for local residents.
3. **Exploring Diversity** identifies lack of understanding as a catalyst for misunderstanding and fear. Inter-Action Belfast discusses its intention to promote both single-identity work and cross-community education.
4. **Highlighting Community Needs** emphasises the importance of publicising the socio-economic needs of interface communities. This policy would secure support for community initiatives, address socio-economic problems and amend deficiencies in the service industry.
5. **Community Safety** prioritises the importance of addressing crime, justice and policing concerns. The section acknowledges the political nature of these concerns, and cites a responsibility to equip community groups with the knowledge, skills and mechanisms necessary to address problems in a comprehensive and strategic manner.
6. **Promoting Participation in Change** discusses the importance of broadening issues of concern and attention. The organisation intends

to manage and disseminate experiences of change and policies of best practice.
7. **Information and Research** explains the importance of providing accurate information and documentation of good practice. This method would assist the wider community in understanding the complex nature of interface dynamics and the process necessary for resolution.

47. Jarman, Neil (2005) *Demography, Development and Disorder: Changing Patterns of Interface Areas.* **Belfast, Community Relations Council.**

This research reviews new and emerging interface areas, while summarising the factors that have contributed to their development. The uneven and sporadic nature of interface violence increases the difficulty of measuring the contributions of specific factors. The study locates a wide variety of interfaces, which exist beyond the boundaries of segregated working-class residential areas. The formalised segregation in Belfast and Derry Londonderry is found to have spread across many towns in Northern Ireland. This research paper redefines interfaces as the intersection of two or more social spaces, which are contested by some or all members of differing ethno-national groups. This competition subsequently transforms unremarkable, previously shared spaces into interfaces. The research concludes that segregation, polarisation and social division are endemic within Northern Ireland, and that these new interfaces have the potential to become sites of recurring violence.

The study examines the effects of social change upon contested spaces. Demographic shifts are acknowledged as increasing tensions in historically quiet areas. Recent demographic changes have increased homogenous single-identity working class communities and subsequently hardened interface lines. The research includes several Belfast examples to support these findings. Suburbanisation has also contributed to growing interface violence. An increasing Catholic population in several suburban areas has accompanied a rise in local tensions. Redevelopment projects, which retain the potential to change local demographics, also contribute to rising community hostility. Any adjustment in demographic patterns affects community relations by shifting established boundaries. The study also looked at the displacement of interface violence from heavily policed areas to neighbouring, unmonitored areas. The role of CCTV and the shifting locations of violence within several communities are also analysed. The research examines the difficulty of maintaining shared spaces and mutually accessible resources throughout Northern Ireland. The effects of seasonal tensions further complicate these efforts.

The role of young people in maintaining interface tension is also examined, along with ongoing clashes between rival school students and the spatial constraints imposed upon young men. The report concludes by encouraging positive and sustained action within neutral spaces, to ensure they remain shared and used by all community members. The complex nature of interface violence is discussed, along with the ongoing displacement of violence.

48. Jarman, Neil (2002) *Managing Disorder: Responding to Interface Violence in North Belfast.* Belfast, Community Development Centre North Belfast.

Chapter One: *Introduction* opens by tracing the history of sectarian violence throughout the city of Belfast, and identifies the summer of 1996 as the most violent period in recent memory. The report explores several important factors that have supported ongoing sectarian violence within Belfast and critiques government policies implemented to counter the problem. The report pays specific attention to the role of young people in community disorder, and places issues of sectarianism and interface violence within a wider social policy context.

Chapter Two: *Violence in North Belfast* provides a detailed account of the violence and disorder in Belfast during 1996. The research argues that sectarian tension and interface violence has become a permanent part of life in many areas. The chapter identifies the existing Belfast interfaces that routinely experience violent disorder. The study criticises police statistics, as the PSNI do not classify sectarian incidents or identify which community was the aggressor/victim, thus hindering attempts to examine patterns of cross-community violence. The study notes a number of factors which have affected the fluctuation of interface violence, such as the Tour of the North parade, the building of several new barriers and the Belfast/Good Friday Agreement, but finds no definitive link between these events and the amount of interface violence. The study establishes interface violence as a continuing and serious problem in Belfast, affected by parades, policing, territory, segregation, power and sectarianism, young people, the Agreement and ambiguity.

Chapter Three: *Interfaces, Barriers and Violence* identifies residential segregation as a prominent feature of urban life in Northern Ireland, and finds that many communities remain highly segregated. The research discusses the variety of marked and unmarked interface areas in Belfast. The study examines the correlation between existing 'peace barriers' and mentality of local community members by outlining the multiple deprivations faced by interface communities. The study finds that physical barriers have had little effect on curtailing violence and disorder.

Chapter Four: *Recreational Rioting* recognises that sectarian clashes are an established feature of life in Northern Ireland, and highlights the prominent involvement of young people in sparking interface violence. Identified as 'recreational rioting' this violence is undertaken from boredom rather than an established political basis, is proving increasingly difficult to control, and contributes to increasingly dangerous sectarian behaviour. The research cites a culture that celebrates and commemorates violence as providing further ideological justification for these forms of anti-social behaviour.

Chapter Five: *Responding to Interface Violence* identifies the historical difficulties of the police service in combating sectarian disorder and explores the merits of wider preventative approaches designed to manage public disorder. The research concludes that mobile phone networks, effective in lowering interface disturbances, have resulted in a positive reduction of serious incidents, but do not have the capacity to tackle all manner of public disorder. The study details the benefits and drawbacks of youth diversion schemes and effects on summer violence. The final section reiterates the difficulties faced by various programmes attempting to confront interface violence. The report identifies the lack of an overall strategy for confronting recurring sectarian interface violence as the largest single hindrance in addressing interface disorder.

Chapter Six: *Police Community Relations* addresses the changes in policing methods in response to the Patten recommendations, describes previous difficulties of parade policing, and the relationship breakdown between police and local communities. The author identifies public order policing as a particularly difficult problem for the police. The section concludes with a genuine sense of uncertainty about the future of police work, and re-iterates the serious obstacles facing police – community relationships.

Chapter Seven: *The Violence in a Wider Context* analyses the history of violence and ceasefires in Northern Ireland. The research concludes that, although the peace process has brought an end to severe violence, it has not ended all sectarian violence and disorder, such as ongoing illegal activities by paramilitary organisations. The section notes an annual rise in domestic violence, racist harassment and anti-social behaviour over the past five years. The research identifies a rise in many forms of violent and sectarian crimes and behaviour in the seven years since the paramilitary ceasefires were declared. The research argues that the lack of adequate policing statistics on sectarian incidents consistently hinders effective responses. The study concludes that attempts to address sectarian incidents must be constructed within a broader framework of rising violent crime and a transforming society.

These study findings are also located in:

Jarman, Neil and O'Halloran, Chris (2001) Recreational Rioting: Young People, Interface Areas and Violence. *Child Care in Practice* Volume 7, Number 1.

Jarman, Neil (2003) Managing Disorder: Responses to Interface Violence in North Belfast. In Owen Hargie and David Dickson (eds) *Researching the Troubles: Social Science Perspectives on the Northern Ireland Conflict.* Edinburgh, Mainstream Publishing.

49. **Jarman, Neil (1999)** *Drawing Back from the Edge: Community Based Responses to Violence in North Belfast.* **Belfast, Community Development Centre North Belfast.**

This report examines the programmes initiated by the Community Development Centre North Belfast, and supported by community activists, to counter interface violence during the summer marching season. The report highlights previous research findings into this topic, including criticism of police responses to contentious situations, the failings of statutory agencies and the inability of communities to accept responsibility for violence. The report cites a breakdown in cross-community communication as perpetuating fear, suspicion, mistrust and violence. The research found that the summer violence had a long-term effect on working class North Belfast, including an increase in residential segregation and a hardening of interface lines.

The report describes the necessity of an interagency statutory group to address the complex needs of displaced families. The CDC and Housing Executive credited the mobile phone network with lowering inter-communal violence in 1997. Interface violence was reduced due to active attempts from paramilitaries and political activists to maintain calm. However, displaced families encountered unnecessary difficulties in dealing with multiple agencies, and the report calls for increased communication and a streamlined process for assisting displaced residents.

It was found that mobile phone holders maintained several important functions during tense situations. Phone holders organised neighbourhood patrols, maintained communication within their area, and held channels of communication into other areas. The two main problems of the mobile phone network were identified as too few phones, and a lack of long-term funding.

50. **Jarman, Neil (ed) (1997)** *On The Edge: Community Perspectives on Civil Disturbances in North Belfast.* **Belfast, Community Development Centre North Belfast.**

This research was initiated by the Community Development Centre as an independent inquiry into the summer violence of 1996. This report analyses the riots and disturbances that took place across North Belfast during the summer, presents evidence from both communities regarding the timeline of events, and highlights possible options for future interventions.

The report presents case studies from a variety of locations across North Belfast. As much of the tensions surrounded Orange Order parading, the report begins by analysing the Tour of the North parade. The report also examines accounts of violence and disorder at Torrens, Clifton Park Avenue, Whitewell/Graymount, Ballysillan/Ligoniel, Skegoneill/Glandore, Duncairn/Limestone, and Mountcollyer. Several recurring themes emerge from these case studies, including disputes over the right to march and the tensions surrounding the Drumcree protests. Additionally, the legacy of sectarian division and intimidating behaviour remained widespread across North Belfast, while cross-community dialogue was virtually non-existent.

The research found that neither side was prepared to acknowledge their share of the blame for specific acts of violence, and consistently blamed the trouble on outside elements, youths or drunks. Both communities were critical of the police, for both being too aggressive and for not intervening early enough when trouble was beginning. This problem was compounded by a lack of political leadership from established politicians.

The report concludes that violence flared for a combination of reasons including rumour, perception, activities of young people, policing methods and lack of communication. The effects of this violence have been a hardening of residential segregation lines, loss of confidence in the police, increased tensions across interface areas and one hundred and ten recognised displaced households. This report also examined the role of the media in the disturbances. Both communities felt misrepresented in media reports, and that media reporting was irresponsible and inflammatory. The report again emphasised the need for cross community dialogue, supported by statutory bodies, to address long-term community tensions.

51. Jarman, Neil and O'Halloran, Chris (2000) *Peacelines or Battlefields: Responding to Violence in Interface Areas.* Belfast, Community Development Centre North Belfast.

This study explores several prominent factors that underpin the emergence and persistence of interface violence, and analyses the attempts being made to counter the problem. The report cites the ongoing problems of low-level violence and residential divisions in interface areas, which have continued despite paramilitary ceasefires and political agreements. The report argues that interface barriers have a limited effect on interface violence, as the clear identification of a boundary can attract people to attack the other community.

The report contends that disputes surrounding parading rights encourage violence, which subsequently raises tension across Northern Ireland. The cyclical nature of the marching season has meant that tensions rise at most interfaces every summer. The report includes short, medium and long-term responses to interface violence. The research maintains that the 1996 violence was fuelled by a breakdown in communication within communities, between communities and through statutory agencies. The mobile phone network has amended this problem by supporting communication between communities. Despite increased communication, the research revealed that many key interface problems were related to young people. Although summer schemes have successfully diverted some young people away from interface areas, acquiring funding for such programmes is difficult. Additionally, the positive results from single-identity community work require substantial funding and hard work. The research concludes that the fragmented nature of interface areas complicates the provision of resources.

The report recommends a specifically targeted response to best address the problems of interface areas. The ongoing lack of resources increases the deprivation of interface communities, while recurring violence and antisocial behaviour require a localised partnership between statutory agencies and community organisations. This study recommends a firm commitment of resources from statutory agencies, along with a more efficient use of existing resources. The research promotes a partnership between statutory, community, governmental and voluntary organisations in supporting local initiatives.

52. Keane, Margaret Christine (1985) *Ethnic Residential Change in Belfast 1969-1977: The Impact of Public Housing Policy in a Plural Society.* Unpublished PhD Thesis, Queens University of Belfast.

Keane's doctorate thesis is an extensive review of housing policies within Belfast during 1969-1977. The research notes an increasing spatial divide between Protestants and Catholics during this period, and finds that public housing policies assisted the two groups in redistributing themselves along ethnic lines. The research identifies three trends in residential segregation, the first being a consolidation of segregated space, followed by clearly defined community boundaries, which has resulted in Catholic segregated space increasing at the expense of mixed housing areas. The study examines the limited opportunities for inter-group contact within segregated areas.

The research examines the impact of the Northern Ireland Housing Executive's Emergency Housing Scheme and Scheme for Purchase of Evacuated Dwellings on polarisation and segregation. Keane finds that segregation increased under these policies until the NIHE unitary policy gradually accepted the existing plurality within society. The study argues that the policies of housing authorities in Belfast since 1969 have directly influenced housing decisions, and subsequently exacerbated polarisation and divisive trends within society.

The study critically analyses NIHE policy between 1969-1977 and finds that the housing authority followed reactive policies to deal with civil disturbances. Protecting existing housing resources, using all available stock and saving money remained NIHE priorities during this time. Keane illustrates how residential segregation was considered thrifty housing management, and permitted the NIHE to avoid a financial crisis.

The thesis concludes that there was no deliberate policy within the NIHE to segregate, but that the organisation is a representative of Northern Irish society which has reflected societal divisions. The study contributes an in-depth analysis of the mechanisms which have influenced the process of residential change and segregation. Keane concludes the research by examining the theoretical implications of NIHE policy and puts forward recommendations for NIHE mixed housing policy.

53. **Kuusisto-Arponen, Anna-Kaisa (2003)** *Our Places - Their Spaces.* Tampere, Tampere University Press.

This academic dissertation examines territoriality within Derry Londonderry. It traces the roots of the Northern Irish conflict, and finds that violence and armed struggle have played a predominant role in the history of Northern Ireland. The research examines socio-spatial organisation in Derry Londonderry and finds that segregation has increased over the last decade and remains a substantial problem. The study presents theories of territoriality, and discusses the boundaries and limits upon social interaction.

The research examines Derry Londonderry in particular and examines ways in which segregation has influenced patterns of social interaction within the city. Segregation is identified as a strategy employed to cope with sectarian violence and conflict, which has evolved as demographic change has occurred. The research examines daily life in Derry Londonderry, and details the complex dynamics of historical influence, segregation and cross-community interaction. The study found that the rise of territorial identity provides security but further stigmatises other groups. The research examines the role of education in perpetuating cross-community contact and finds that the educational system reinforces social segregation.

The recent emergence of intra-communal warfare is examined, along with security arrangements and policing structures in Northern Ireland. The study found that the contemporary peace process has created a new societal situation where traditional sources of authority are fragmenting, and more competition exists to control local communities. The ongoing violence within Derry Londonderry is analysed, and the 'ghetto mentality' is examined. It is found that a sense of place provides personal, communal and territorial identity to individuals. The study concludes by tracing the evolution of political culture in Northern Ireland, and examines the different types of coping strategies employed by residents to withstand conflict and hostile social situations.

54. **Lenadoon Community Forum (2003)** *Lenadoon Community Forum, 1992-2002.* Belfast, Lenadoon Community Forum.

The Lenadoon Community Forum was established to address the social and economic needs of the Lenadoon estate. This publication describes the two five-year community plans for the area. The local community has been deeply affected by the 'Troubles' and the organisation aims to improve the standard of living for all residents. This forum was established because of community frustration with the Belfast Action Team. The first five-year development plan for the Lenadoon Community Forum (1992-1999) targeted unemployment, young people, tenant participation, environmental strategy, human resources and economic development. The report includes specific details about the programmes and funding for each of these target areas.

The Lenadoon Community Forum development plan for 1999-2004 targets health and well-being, children and young people, housing and the interface, education and employment and community infrastructure. The report describes the effect of paramilitary ceasefires and the subsequent peace process upon local community development. The report emphasises the importance of mental health and counselling services for local residents. The report concludes that the recent social and economic improvements, which have benefited many communities, have not materialised in Lenadoon. The report questions the future availability of funding from the EU and local agencies.

55. **McEldowney, Malachy; Sterrett, Ken and Gaffikin Frank (2001) Architectural Ambivalence: the Built Environment and Cultural Identity in Belfast. In William Neill and Hanns-Uve Schwedler (eds)** *Urban Planning and Cultural Inclusion: Lessons from Belfast and Berlin.* **Basingstoke, Palgrave.**

This article traces the relationship between identity and ambivalence in Belfast's built environment as it evolved from the early 19th century to the present day. The publication considers if it is now necessary for Belfast to look forwards, rather than backwards, and if the city can possibly build for peace, rather than war. It describes the Northern Irish political history as full of meanings, which have created the built environment and endowed it with symbolism. The research traces the residential and commercial growth of Belfast, and finds that certain locations reflected almost exclusive Protestant ownership of commerce and political power. The study finds that the environment of Belfast formerly served a commercial purpose and a political-cultural role by supporting a renewed political order and sense of identity across Protestant class interests. The overall restructuring of Belfast during the 1960s caused a large social upheaval in many working-class areas. This process of modernisation was abandoned in the early 1970s due to political violence and subsequently caused de-population in city areas.

The authors examine the NIHE's new designs for working-class areas, which have incorporated 'defensible space' into design plans and consider the physical and visual damage suffered by the city centre during the IRA bombing campaign. A series of initiatives designed to revitalise the city centre were implemented, along with an ideological offensive to counter Belfast's international image. The research discusses the active decisions to encourage all new buildings to appear modern, rather than old-fashioned, in order to show confidence in the future. The study relays concerns over this loss of Victorian identity in an attempt to transcend local conflict. The reasons for the slow conservation movement are discussed, along with the willingness of the Nationalist community to 'adopt' buildings such as City Hall and Stormont. The research examines how 'old' buildings refer backwards in time, and Belfast's problems involve people preoccupied with looking backwards in time. Buildings which emphasised looking forward were considered necessary. The research argues that the loss of local identity was an unnecessary price to pay for imposed normality. The section closes by noting the feeling that new, modern buildings will survive and exist in a context of peace.

The article discusses the usage of 'peace lines' and different design variations, and concludes that these barriers symbolise an increasing acceptance of segregation in public housing areas. It concludes that Belfast urban design reflects a loss of local confidence and international modern trends. Regarding identity, the research concludes that Belfast has looked backwards and forwards simultaneously. The study concludes that the current challenge facing urban planners is to design for inclusively.

56. Moore, Ruth and Smyth, Marie (1996) *Two Policy Papers: Policing and Sectarian Division; Urban Regeneration and Sectarian Division.* **Derry, Templegrove Action Research Limited.**

This publication addresses multiple aspects of residential segregation found in Derry Londonderry. The first paper, entitled Policing and Sectarian Division, discusses the difficulties faced in policing divided areas and enclave communities. The study emphasises the need for a police force accepted by both communities and free from political ideologies. Policing and Sectarian Division provides a background to policing in Northern Ireland, and argues that the future policing service must specifically address factors relating to sectarian division and residential segregation. In order to effectively address policing in segregated areas, policy and training are needed at all levels of the service. The report describes policing as a security force policing an emergency and recommends a strategy to address the religious discrepancy within the RUC.

The second paper contains a number of recommendations to further the regeneration process of Derry Londonderry and emphasises the case for special attention and support for deprived communities and enclave areas. Residential Segregation and Enclave Communities describes the pattern of increasing residential segregation in Derry Londonderry. The report examines the significance of settlement patterns in relation to policing, indicating that certain areas have become 'no-go' areas for the RUC, and discusses the attitudes of enclave communities towards policing. Both communities remain concerned that officers are unaware of local problems and RUC officers remain reluctant to construct a good working relationship with the community. The report addresses the specific community concerns of interface areas around the Fountain and Gobnascale. Intimidation towards enclave areas is often perceived as a threat to the entire community. The difference in policing problems between the two communities is explained by the differences in political identities. This report concludes that the needs and concerns of all communities must be taken into account in the strategic planning of policing practices.

57. Murtagh, Brendan (2002) *The Politics of Territory: Policy and Segregation in Northern Ireland.* **Basingstoke, Palgrave.**

Chapter 3: *Segregation, Territory and Policy:* examines the nature of ethno-religious segregation in Northern Ireland and discusses future policy decisions regarding segregation and territoriality. The study examines the difficulties confronting urban planners regarding territoriality and land-development projects and concludes that policy-makers must factor the spatial dynamics of Northern Ireland into all future development programmes. Murtagh examines previous geographic, anthropological and social science research that emphasises a link between spatial segregation and lack of contact, understanding and knowledge of the 'out-group'. This finding is correlated with widening social distance and minimising opportunities for beneficial contact. The report analyses the Northern Ireland Housing Executive's role in sustaining residential segregation. The research quotes a NIHE policy document that discusses the difficulties of promoting integrated housing and the need to protect freedom of tenant choice.

Murtagh also provides an in-depth review of previous studies that examine a variety of rural community interactions. Although the section details a numerous array of findings, all evidence indicates a strong level of existing tensions within rural communities. The evidence indicates an ongoing 'rural repopulation', with a fifteen percent increase in the Catholic population. The section describes the Protestant community's response to this demographic change as engaging in a degree of residential adjustment, and consciously attempting to maintain previous attitudes. The section concludes that 'rural re-population' has exacerbated political and territorial cleavages in a number of areas.

Chapter 4: *Life on the Interface:* examines the origins of 'peace lines', summarises statistical findings, and analyses the response of policy makers within the planning system to specific interface problems in Northern Ireland. This report argues that the direct and indirect costs of peace fences are minimal compared to the impact on local residents. High levels of unemployment, deprivation and isolation within interface communities are cited to support the argument. The chapter describes the role of the Northern Ireland Housing Executive toward interface housing policy, and concludes that this agency does not provide a coherent policy response to these difficulties. The NIHE acknowledge their role as peace line builders, but cite that the decision to build lies with the Northern Ireland Office. The Department of the Environment perceives interfaces as spatial manifestations of the structure of Northern Ireland's divided society. The research cites three case studies: Duncairn Gardens, Alliance/Glenbryn and Springvale, which demonstrate the DENI's approach to interface communities. The analysis reveals three integral themes to DENI policy namely 'wedge planning', encouraging community participation and creating local cross-community infrastructure.

The research also demonstrates NIHE's recognition of security concerns in certain areas and concludes that buffer zones have begun to emerge between conflicting groups, which correlates with DENI's 'wedge' approach. After examining two case studies, the research concludes that NIHE housing management interests are less concerned with preservation of ethnic territory, and more concerned with managing stock to ensure maximum financial return. Case studies from Woodburn, Ballynafeigh and Extern provide examples of successful community based initiatives. The research supports this style of programme, as it addresses local issues rather than implementing broad policy objectives. The research concludes by reiterating the variety of approaches designed to address interface problems. The study confirms that DENI and NIHE initiatives have formalised ethno-religious boundaries, while community initiatives have reduced local tension. The inevitable decline of some populations will force the Housing Executive to make difficult decisions in the future. The study warns that any attempt to produce a strategic framework for Northern Ireland must recognise the context of divisions, the priority of integrated housing and the need to respect segregation and personal choice.

58. Murtagh, Brendan (1999) *Community and Conflict in Rural Ulster.* Coleraine, Centre for the Study of Conflict.

The study investigates community relations attitudes and behaviours in rural Ulster, explores the presence of rural interfaces and presents implications for community relations policy in Northern Ireland. The areas targeted for research all report high levels of rural violence, experiences of dramatic population shift and established 'high conflict' areas. The research suggests an increase of sectarian practices within rural areas and the importance of land ownership is identified as a key variable in rural community relations. The study examines recent demographic differences at the rural ward level, and concludes that Protestant residents more commonly engage in a degree of residential adjustment. The study examines the demographic changes as a continually reducing Protestant population and an increasing Catholic population. The demographic trends also show a proportionate increase in the Catholic population in South Armagh and a proportionate increase in the Protestant population in the north of the study area, which has a profound effect on the interface community. The section concludes that the overall study area of Armagh is highly segregated, with only 7 of the 32 wards being mixed, and a generally poor social and economic profile.

The research scrutinises mutually exclusive patterns of behaviour, common identity and overall patterns of social behaviour to illustrate the complexities and contradictions of rural Ulster. The research presents further qualitative data, which shows that the attitudes among both Protestants and Catholics are more extreme in the study area than among all rural dwellers and Northern Ireland as a whole. Murtagh argues that the history and experience of violence, along with the sense of community sustainability, are the specific variables explaining this segregated attitude.

The research examines the importance of territory at the micro-community level. Two villages were selected for focused analysis, and the research confirmed the near-complete segregation of the two villages. A sharp contrast was found between the perceptions of respondents regarding community relations within and between the two villages. While community relations in the two villages are perceived to be good, community relations between the two villages were described as poor. The importance of avoidance appears to be a key variable. The religious split in the use of services has always been a feature of community life in this part of rural Armagh. Speculation about the role of Nationalists in sectarian murders fuelled sectarian fear and suspicion, and remains deeply ingrained in the Protestant psyche. This section concludes by summarising the negative effects of sectarian attacks on local security, safety, education, economy and commerce. The research suggests that a dual force is at work, as the local population is being eroded both by natural population decline and by the detrimental impact of physical attacks. The study addresses the history of rural land transfer as an ongoing segregated system. The study identifies principal gatekeepers (such as auctioneers and solicitors) who directly influence land sales, and comments that this closed system fuels scrutiny and suspicion while allowing corrupt and sectarian practices to continue unabated. Recently, this difficulty has been eased by long-term lease agreements rather than the outright selling of land, and the study reiterates the importance of land and housing in Northern Ireland.

The study advocates amending rural and urban regeneration by making community relations a central objective, and illustrates the slow response of certain community sectors to these issues. The study concludes by reiterating three broad ideas, namely: the establishment of a special commission to address the issue of territoriality and the relationship between local violence and the nature of conflict, the relationship between territoriality and the nature of conflict, and the need for community relations practitioners to adjust their practices to best meet the needs of residents.

59. Murtagh, Brendan (1995) Image Making Versus Reality: Ethnic Division and the Planning Challenge of Belfast's Peace Lines. In William Neill, Diana Fitzsimons and Brendan Murtagh (eds) *Reimaging the Pariah City: Urban Development in Belfast & Detroit.* Aldershot, Avebury.

This chapter describes the spatial problems created by ethnic division, and proposes new approaches to land-use planning. The research explains the severity and complexity of ethnic division in the Belfast urban area, and describes the challenges facing land-use planners regarding land and housing facilities. The chapter profiles daily life in interface communities, and examines three case-study areas. These show high levels of deprivation compounded by proximity to the interface. In summary, Murtagh argues that interface communities suffer higher levels of poverty than any other areas in Northern Ireland, endure restricted access to necessary services and facilities and remain unable to encourage economic development. The article goes on to measure attitudes towards one's 'own' and the 'other' community, and acknowledges community fears regarding loss of territory and community stability.

The study continues by examining the implications of ethnic division upon land-use policy. Murtagh advocates three principles for urban planning within interface communities, and describes alternative approaches to defining spatial problems, and addressing the urban divide. The study encourages amending strategy, skills, policy systems and planning functions.

- **Strategy:** argues that the nature of the urban problem calls for a new approach in survey work, and lists potential considerations. The article calls for all future strategies to address the physical, economic and social development of interface areas. The author advocates the inclusion of a community relations strategy in planning initiatives.
- **Skills:** encourages further education regarding divided areas for Belfast urban planners. This education would equip planners with community relations skills and initiatives suited to land-use planning.
- **Policy Systems:** identifies the important relationship between community relations and land development. The author encourages all major decisions and planning application to be subject to an ethnic impact assessment.
- **Style:** emphasises that all plans must be multi-dimensional in nature and incorporate planning, community relations, public participation, anti-poverty policies and environmental considerations. This formula would encourage new ways of thinking regarding land use and social problems in Belfast.

This article concludes by discussing the important role of land-use planning in improving the Belfast urban environment. The chapter emphasises the necessity of re-defining the content, scope and style of current local planning strategies.

60. Murtagh, Brendan (1994) *Ethnic Space and the Challenge to Land Use Planning: A Survey of Belfast's Peace Lines.* Jordanstown, Centre for Policy Research.

This research examines the physical, social and demographic profiles of interface areas and concludes that ongoing difficulties present a range of inter-linked problems. The author calls for regeneration based on analysis and understanding of local problems, and a recognition between land use planning and community relations. The work establishes the long history of ethnic territoriality in Belfast. Recent research shows urban segregation sharpening, especially among lower socio-economic groups and those who live in public sector housing. The research implies that Protestants and Catholics share many commonalities regarding lifelong opportunities when they reside in public-sector housing. The central challenge to any planning statement will be ensuring that sustainable inter-group contact is a realistic possibility in areas with intense inter-group fractures. The research then discusses the high financial, human and image costs of peace barriers.

The research finds that the Northern Ireland Housing Executive has no established response to over-arching interface problems, except recognising the security concerns in these areas. This report argues that housing managers share well-defined objectives in managing and controlling their stock in a way that will maximise rental income and minimise costs. However, interface difficulties prevent these objectives from being realised. These statutory agencies are described as being less concerned with preservation of ethnic territory and more concerned with managing stock to ensure maximum economic return. The research then examines the different policies of the Department of the Environment and the Housing Executive to interface areas, and concludes that the 'buffer zone' policy has become the preferred strategy of the Department of the Environment. However, certain community initiatives have demonstrated that conflict negotiation and resolution can be used to effect positive change in some communities.

The report also examines life on the interface, and suggests that peace line communities experience multiple deprivations. This research shows that the types of deprivation, such as unemployment, low levels of income and benefit dependency, are compounded by proximity to an interface. Additionally, interfaces directly affect community movement and interaction. The research finds that the majority of people living on an interface have a positive attitude towards the out-group, but that cross-community initiatives can be severely restricted by extremists within the community. The report calls for a coordinated action programme, which takes into account the unique dynamics of an interface community, within the framework of a land planning agenda.

The study discusses the implications of the research findings for future planning and housing policies, and projects a series of options for consideration. The research advocates maintaining a strong link between community relations and development proposals. The Housing Executive is named as the best-placed organization to carry out specific policy development. The study emphasises the need for a new way of thinking about and responding to specific spatial problems. The report concludes that strong psychological factors underpin the need to live among people who share a common identity. This pattern of segregation has increased over time, and subsequent contact between Protestants and Catholics has decreased. This finding focuses attention on theorised positive benefits of intergroup contact. The research finds that interface areas and peace barriers create significant financial, human and image costs for local areas, and that significant and sustainable inter-group contact is necessary to have a positive impact on the quality of life in interface areas.

These findings are also presented in:

Murtagh, Brendan (1999) *Ethnic Space and the Challenge to Land Use Planning: A Survey of Belfast's Peace Lines.* Belfast, Community Relations Council.

61. Neill, William (1998) *Whose City? Can a Place Vision for Belfast Avoid the Issue of Identity?* Belfast, Queen's University of Belfast.

This research explores the ongoing struggle of power relations in Belfast, and finds that symbols of past dominance have become increasingly politically and psychologically sensitive since the signing of the Good Friday/Belfast Agreement. The study examines how identity issues have become incorporated into urban planning, and provides an in-depth analysis of Stormont symbolism. The publication concludes by challenging urban planners about consistently avoiding ethnic identity and spatial concerns.

Section One: *Place Vision and Place Identity* examines urban development within contested areas across Europe, and explores the relationship between place and identity formation. Theoretical propositions regarding group identification in urban planning are discussed.

Section Two: *A New Place Vision for Belfast* discusses the regeneration and development planned for Belfast in the wake of the paramilitary ceasefires and the role of the Department of the Environment in managing tensions between developing areas. The study acknowledges a positive development by political leaders in agreeing upon a 'Vision Response' for strategic planning in Belfast. This supports bringing issues of representational space and ethnic identities into the centre of place visioning for Belfast. The author argues that planning exercises regarding

Belfast should not be avoided because of controversy and difficulties.

Section Three: *Reading Stormont* examines the political and symbolic importance of this political institution. A core issue of the Northern Ireland Peace Process concerned the identity of the Nationalist Catholic population and how expressions of identity can become officially legitimised and facilitated. These concerns become a spatial planning issue as identities have a direct relationship to place and surroundings. The research argues that the contentious image of the Stormont Assembly is unlikely to gain general acceptance, as it symbolises self-assertion and the will to preserve British cultural identity. The study concludes that Stormont continues to exist as an apex of Protestant representational space, and as a symbol of defiance against Irish Catholic nationalism. These concerns have remained ignored by many planners, and have left an unmediated gulf between rival ethnic claims.

Section Four: *Urban Design and Memory* examines the design of Belfast City Centre as politically neutral territory, and discusses several contentious issues of symbolism and cultural expression. The issue of place naming identifies a perception of Irish-language signs as a marker of territory. A study of cultural quarters identifies Catholic West Belfast as a unique expression of cultural identity. The study of parades is defined as disagreement over symbolic marking of territory. The study finds that the role of parades, to demonstrate Unionist identity, has become more important since the closure of Stormont.

Section Five: *Conclusions* finds that the issue of a divided city was not addressed in planning documents for Northern Ireland, due to the government normalisation strategy to downplay the existence of conflict. It is hoped that planning autonomy and freedom will follow devolution. As recent consultation reports fail to promote a planning process based on the recognition of real conflicts, the study calls for real planning compromises as part of an enduring peace settlement. The research concludes that planners should incorporate a more inclusive representational Belfast landscape that recognises both cultural traditions.

62. Neill, William (1995) **Lipstick on the Gorilla? Conflict Management, Urban Development and Image Making in Belfast.** In William Neill, Diana Fitzsimons and Brendan Murtagh (eds) *Reimaging the Pariah City: Urban Development in Belfast & Detroit.* Aldershot, Avebury.

Neill's article begins by acknowledging the importance of image marketing for cities in order to attract tourism and spur economic growth. The article examines the history and policy formation of image-based urban planning in Belfast and considers the implications for sectarian and class divisions.

Section One: *Localities and Rationales for Re-Imaging* presents both sides of the debate regarding the ability of regional governments to retain control during restructuring. The research notes trends towards modernisation of arts and culture industries, local heritage and physical renewal of the city centre during re-imaging, and includes examples from Newcastle-Upon-Tyne, Glasgow and Birmingham. The study finds mixed reaction to re-imaging. The possibility for sharp divisions between core and commuter workers, along with an increase of civic pride and employment are discussed.

Section Two: *Image and Planning in Belfast: The Policy* identifies a strong hands-on political influence in Belfast planning decisions and categorises the Department of the Environment (DoE) as monopolizing planning policy and primarily focused on the cultivation of a neutral and normal city centre. The research recognises the unique re-imaging problems facing Belfast, and identifies the DoE approach as a strategy of normalisation and economic promotion, in order to counter unflattering perceptions. The section goes on to trace important periods of urban development between the 1970s and 1990s.

- **Defensive policy of the 1970s** describes the tough defensive security throughout the city centre. The construction of the Westlink is attributed to cutting off the city centre from riotous and disorderly areas.
- **Encouragement of tentative recovery 1980-84** attributes the growth of the city centre to changes in political tactics during the Troubles. This change permitted a relaxation of city centre security restrictions, and encouraged development and financial support.
- **Active promotion and planning 1985-94** discusses the major initiatives of the Belfast Urban Area Plan, designed to promote normality within the city. This policy emphasises the relationship between physical planning and economic development and the role both could play in managing the difficult political process and resolving problems. The research notes how Belfast city centre became harnessed as a symbol for a normal Northern Ireland.

Section Three: *Aspects of Policy Formation* discusses three overlapping concerns which hindered urban planning and development in Belfast
- **A Structural Bind** concludes that two clashing cultural identities lie at the core of Northern Ireland, which is subject to a structural bind, where the fundamental interests of one community can be secured only at the expense of the fundamental interests of the other.
- **Concentration of Power** discusses the planning and decision-making power within the Department of the Environment. The section concludes that debates on policy planning are restricted as the DoE retains a substantial monopoly of urban planners and building contracts.
- **Urban Privatism** describes Belfast as a testing ground for the Conservative Government's economic policy. According to the research, this emphasis on private investment and ownership has not assisted deprived communities.

Section Four: *Class and Sectarianism - Is planning really so neutral?* argues that the government's economic policy is not neutral regarding class, rather the main beneficiaries of the Belfast reimaging process are the middle classes, while few policies exist for deprived areas. The research identifies the main difficulties of re-imaging as its property-led focus and inability to address deprived areas. The section continues by arguing that sectarian relations limit policy implementation, and that Belfast remains burdened by sectarian symbols. The section concludes that the concentration on superficial changes has not addressed deep ethnic antagonisms.

This article concludes that, because of class and sectarian limiting factors, planning for neutrality in Belfast has inherent weaknesses as a strategy for conflict management. The report emphasises the necessity of an agreement regarding urban design and the role of public art in Belfast, which reflects the city's cross community cultural heritage. The author concludes that Belfast needs to be re-imagined, not superficially re-imaged.

63. **North Belfast Community Action Project (2002)** *Report of the Project Team.* **Belfast, NBCAP.**

This publication explores social and community issues in North Belfast and recommends a number of measures to combat violence and deprivation. The report outlines the direct and indirect costs of failing to address community problems, and calls for North Belfast to receive urgent special treatment.

Part One: *Analysis of the Issues* summarises the numerous disadvantages within North Belfast. The ongoing inter-community violence and lack of cohesion receives specific attention. The Project envisages joint initiatives across many government agencies and an eventual creation of vibrant and sustainable community infrastructure.

- **Socio-Economic Profile** provides population, employment and educational statistics for the area. The study notes a large population of young people, high rates of unemployment and benefit dependency but finds no immediate correlation between unemployment and deprivation and population decline.
- **Territoriality** examines near-complete community segregation in North Belfast, where the majority of communities are regarded as exclusively Protestant or Catholic. This ongoing divide harms community relations and limits shared access to facilities. The section concurs with NIHE policy that integrated living cannot occur until community relations are restored.
- **Sectarianism and Interfaces** discusses the scarce resources available for confronting sectarian attitudes. The report defines sectarianism as a system of distorted and destructive patterns of relating, which is generated and sustained by antagonised religious and political divisions. The patchwork nature of North Belfast communities makes conflict likely and avoidance impossible. The perceptions of security barriers, the lack of access to resources and ongoing low-level violence around interface areas are discussed. The role of young people in perpetuating interface violence is examined.
- **Political Leadership** calls for elected representatives to provide leadership that rises above intense emotion within some

communities. The study puts forward a shared vision for problem solving and peace building, which would combat street-level problems. The role of political leaders in addressing the harmful impact of paramilitary control is discussed.
- **Community Capacity in North Belfast** finds that the level of community capacity varies widely between areas. Although each community suffers in different ways and to different levels, each community encounters difficulties in accessing project funding. The study finds community capacity building essential for long-term development in North Belfast.
- **Youth** attributes youth-related problems to a scarcity of resources and facilities and resultant boredom, rather than malicious intent. The Project calls for more resources to assist young people who leave school without qualifications. The study advocates an increase in numbers, staff and funding for all youth programmes in North Belfast.
- **Health Issues** identifies three major health issues harming North Belfast. Young people and substance abuse is identified as a prominent problem, along with mental health difficulties and rising suicide rates.

Part Two: *Summary of Analysis* clarifies the research findings. The report states that there is little chance of improving standards without collaborative participation in the planning process. There is no current sense of strategic or shared vision for North Belfast. The study identifies the need for a large-scale physical regeneration project in the area, and concludes that no single agency or organization can deliver comprehensive improvement.

Part Three: *Action Initiated by the Project* describes both the completed and ongoing community work supported by the Project.

Part Four: *Recommended Further Action* proposes an integrated plan shared between Government agencies, community organisations and local residents to address interface issues, boost community capacity, improve economic, social and cultural life, and examine health and education concerns. The Project recommends establishing a dedicated, well-funded unit to address the problems in North Belfast, and delineates the power and structure of the unit. The four main functions of the unit are identified as building community capacity, creating an overall strategy, building partnership and addressing interface issues.
- **Community Capacity Building** recommends £3 million additional funding for community capacity building, to be drawn from the proposed Community Empowerment Partnership.

- **A New Development Site for North Belfast** addresses the need for a large-scale physical regeneration project in the area.
- **Centre for Citizenship** calls for a centre in North Belfast to promote learning about citizenship and the related concepts of rights and obligations.
- **Health** supports a reconfiguring of service delivery to better meet the needs of the area.
- **Education** recommends additional resources to be made available for supporting links between schools, pupils and parents.
- **New Approaches** supports providing Internet communication and music resources for North Belfast residents to develop non-confrontational, cross-community contact.

64. Northern Ireland Housing Executive (2000) *The North Belfast Housing Strategy: Tackling Housing Needs.* **Belfast, Northern Ireland Housing Executive.**

This strategy document addresses housing difficulties within the North Belfast area and contains a seven-year, £133m strategy for improving housing and community conditions. The Housing Executive attributes sectarianism and segregation as detrimental to meeting housing demand, and discusses the impracticality of Executive-administered territorial adjustments to North Belfast. The goal for this publication is to recognise the fundamental right to good housing and create a strategy that can be delivered.

The report identifies the different types of need within Catholic and Protestant communities. The Executive sets three challenges for itself: to meet housing needs, improve housing conditions and place housing strategies within inter-agency policies. Five interlinked components to the Housing Executive plan are also highlighted: to increase housing supply, make better use of existing stock, improve conditions of current Housing Executive stock, sustain and improve private housing areas, and promote regeneration and social inclusion through partnerships.

The cornerstone of the North Belfast strategy is identified as meeting housing needs. The difficulties of segregation and territoriality have made the housing market extremely inefficient, subsequently hindering the implementation of Housing Executive objectives. Seven major influences that shape strategic planning context for North Belfast are identified. The impact of demographic change and subsequent effects upon housing stock are also acknowledged. The current social waiting list trends and the inadequate responses to urgent housing need are discussed. The section details the Housing Executive's perception of deprivation, social exclusion and long-term poverty in the target area. The scarcity of available house stock for urgent need cases is highlighted. The difficulties surrounding land-use planning and territorial control are discussed, with the Executive identifying a substantial development capacity in North Belfast. The theme of an increasing demand for single-person households runs throughout the chapter, along with the difficulties of the segregated nature of housing availability in North Belfast.

The report outlines a detailed response to these problems. These include making better use of available stock, improving current stock through physical and social regeneration schemes, sustaining and improving private housing facilities, accessing the private rented sector to facilitate single-person homes, using the private rented sector to reduce waiting lists, promoting area-based renewal and promoting regeneration and social inclusion through partnerships. The strategy anticipates reducing the overall housing waiting list by half, while paying special attention to urgent need cases, especially family urgent-need cases. The waiting time differences between Catholic and Protestant families, it is anticipated, should soon be eroded, along with removing housing condition differentials.

65. Officer, David (2001) *Towards a Community Relations Strategy for Donegall Pass.* **Belfast, University of Ulster.**

This report measures the impact and development of community relations activities in Donegall Pass and contains recommendations to enhance these programmes. The report begins by presenting an in-depth research methodology and cites the unique nature of a community-led community relations strategy.

Section Two: *South Belfast: The Social and Economic Context in Perspective* identifies a wide variety of social and economic living standards in South Belfast. The drastic changes in local dynamics have continually hindered the creation of social cohesion and an improvement in community relations. The study examines the significance of the Special Support Programme for Peace and Reconciliation, which aims to reinforce progress towards a peaceful and stable society through a variety of projects. The report identifies how several community development projects have been denied necessary funding, which is detrimental to the area. The section identifies a steep decline in population, changes in existing social composition and experiences of violence. The research highlights substantial social problems due to unemployment, demographics and paramilitary presence. The aims and objectives of the Donegall Pass Community Forum are discussed, along with significant outcomes of the project.

Section Three: *Donegall Pass and Community Relations* identifies the Donegall Pass community as occupying an isolated position inside South Belfast. The history and current relations between Donegall Pass and neighbouring communities are discussed, along with intra-community relations between Donegall Pass minority communities. The research fails to identify any long-term community relations project in the area, but the evidence suggests potential for building upon existing relationships in the area.

Section Four: *Towards a Strategic Plan* describes a number of core elements which constitute a basis for a future community strategic plan and discusses ways to sustain community identity while building on cross-community relationships and sustaining existing community relations. The role of the South Belfast Partnership Board is analysed, and the research recommends the Donegall Pass Community Forum to engage with the Board to aid in the creation of a community relations strategy. This process would ensure that the peace-building strategy is an inter-agency, inter-sectoral policy.

66. Persic, Callie (2004) *The State of Play*. Belfast, Inter-Action Belfast.

Section One: *Introduction* details the history of trauma in interface areas and discusses the increased attention paid to interface areas during the recent peace process. This report provides an analysis of many important issues affecting West Belfast, including territoriality, sectarianism, and political leadership. The study notes that sectarianism is widespread across Northern Ireland, but it is often only at interfaces where tensions evolve into violence. The report provides evidence of increasing segregation and intolerance between Catholics and Protestants, and argues that the peace process cannot be successful as long as interfaces remain acceptable venues for displays of sectarian behaviour. The report aims to clarify the current levels of deprivation along the Springfield interface and analyse the complex issues facing interface communities.

Section Two: *The Creation of Interfaces* analyses the history of segregation and single-identity areas, and examines the personal and financial costs of maintaining barriers. The report identifies the typical characteristics of interface areas as barren waste areas. The report explores the history of Springfield interfaces by charting the numbers of deaths and violent activities in the community. Twelve current flashpoint areas along the Springfield road are identified. The section offers an explanation for the numerous causes of interface violence. The section concludes by examining the deprivation levels of interface communities.

- **Community Space** identifies territory as having both pragmatic and symbolic importance in Belfast. Residential segregation is shown to be a long-standing feature of the city, which maintains sectarianism and violence and keeps interface communities separated yet interlocked. The cost of duplicating resources is also discussed.
- **Parades** explores the existing community tensions surrounding parades and marches. The report includes both sides of the theoretical parade debate, and identifies positive developments regarding parading along the Springfield Road.
- **Sectarianism** examines the existence of sectarian attitudes across Northern Ireland, and identifies interfaces as promoting visible divisions.
- **Fears, Rumours and Uncertainty** describes interface living as characterised by unpredictability, day-to-day survival and crisis management. Due to the mistrust between communities, rumours spread quickly across areas and this requires specific programmes and interventions.
- **Violence** examines the effects of violent behaviour upon interface communities.
- **Youth-led Violence** explores the concept of 'recreational rioting' as a catalyst for interface violence and the prevalence of anti-social behaviour in the nearby vicinity of security barriers.

Section Three: *Socio-Economic Profile* examines provisions available for the substantial minority of young people living in interface communities. It also reports severe deprivation among interface residents, and calls for strategic and long-term action to combat poverty, social exclusion and multiple deprivations.

Section Four: *The Spark* discusses the new approach adopted by the Springfield Inter-Community Development Project towards conflict resolution. The group identify a need for a community development strategy, which would facilitate a forum for community representatives to discuss issues of joint concern. The forum places foremost the rights of individuals and the community to influence decisions, and emphasises participation by capitalizing upon existing skills and community ownership of the process. It examines the history and leadership of the project, the political context and sensitivity of the project.

Section Five: *Towards the Future* examines the importance of responsible political leadership, the necessity of community ownership of the project, and defines the responsibilities of ex-combatants. Future plans include active steps towards community development across the interface, and emphasizing community safety, exploring diversity and disseminating information and research findings.

67. Robinson, Peter (2002) *Victims: The Story of Unionists 'Living' at the Interface with Republican Short Strand.* Belfast, Democratic Unionist Party.

This publication outlines the DUP's perspective on the sectarian violence along the inner east interface during the summer of 2002. Robinson sets out the Unionist case to provide greater understanding of the community conflict. The history of violence along the interface, along with residential movement and subsequent deprivation of the area is discussed. The publication includes accusations of a Republican agenda, and the Republican need to maintain violence and tensions for political reasons. The report depicts an ongoing media bias against Unionist residents. Both the physical damage to homes and the psychological harm to residents due to ongoing interface violence are reported. Robinson sharply criticises the policing of the interface, and concludes that the sustained violence is a method of ethnic cleansing

68. Shirlow, Peter (2001) *Fear and Ethnic Division. Peace Review*, Vol. 13 No. 1.

This paper examines the basis for community fear, and analyses the effect of fear upon 'normalised' patterns of work, shopping, leisure and habitation. The research illustrates the manifestation of animosity, mistrust and division due to residential segregation. Shirlow argues that existing residential segregation regulates ethno-sectarian violence, while separating members of Protestant and Catholic communities. This report examines the localised politics of territorial control and resistance that subsequently reject ideas of assimilation and shared space and examines the ability of physical peace barriers to protect politically opposed communities.

According to the research, fear of intimidation encourages residents to relocate within segregated communities. The study examines how this current mosaic of 'opposing' communities creates distinct 'safe' and 'unsafe' areas for local residents. The research analyses the effects of segregation on deprived interface communities. Despite similar deprivation levels, Protestant and Catholic interface communities rarely share neighbourhood facilities. Shirlow identifies the fear of being attacked as a majority factor in determining mobility.

The paper concludes that interface areas remain split along religious lines, which subsequently restricts mobility. The climate of victimisation and besiegement subsequently limits attempts at cross-community contact. The existing fear and mistrust instead perpetuate a desire for communal separation while recent political improvements have not improved cross-community attitudes within segregated communities.

69. Shirlow, Peter (1998) *Fear, Mobility and Living in the Ardoyne and Upper Ardoyne.* **Coleraine, University of Ulster.**

This study analyses the relationship between community threat and personal mobility. Survey results provide an understanding of besiegement and the effects upon job-seeking, economic reconstruction, leisure time and consumption. The report examines the complex effects of different forms of violence, and suggests that the pervasive culture of fear creates socio-economic losses in the retail, service and industrial sectors of North Belfast. The study addresses the existence of these concerns in the Ardoyne and Upper Ardoyne communities, and conveys the localised nature of politics, territorial control, avoidance and resistance, which have resulted in communal differences, segregation and exclusion.

The research finds that experience of violence and fear affect people of all ages, knowledge of fear and victimhood are passed on through generations and this type of communication is a major factor in the reproduction of violence and apprehension. The Ardoyne and Upper Ardoyne are experiencing dissimilar patterns of growth, household structure and housing demand, which subsequently affect communal relations. Another outcome of sectarian violence has been the continual movement of individuals in search of a safe place to live and the research reports a sizeable minority of Ardoyne and Upper Ardoyne residents who relocated due to fear or intimidation.

The study examines the link between employment, intimidation and personal security, Within the sample, a vast majority of Ardoyne respondents, compared to a minority of Upper Ardoyne respondents, indicated that employment decisions are influenced by fear. These factors contribute to high unemployment rates within the area. The research also discovered a notable decline in the numbers of residents working in either mixed workplaces or workplaces 'dominated' by the other religion.

Additionally, while Ardoyne residents were more likely to have experienced intimidation within the workplace, both communities were hesitant about travelling to work through areas dominated by the other community. The section concludes that fear of workplace intimidation and travelling through certain areas has facilitated a significant drop in mixed-religion workplaces for local residents.

The next section of the research analyses the effects of fear on everyday expenditure patterns. The vast majority of respondents chose to shop in areas defined as either Protestant/Unionist or Catholic/Nationalist, but the majority of respondents fraternise in places used by members of the other religion at least once a month. This suggests that many respondents do not, in terms of their socialising, continually advocate 'avoidance strategies'. Only distinct minorities of respondents from both communities were prepared to socialise in facilities dominated by the 'other' religion. This section concludes that, although people patronise mixed places, this does not necessarily create meaningful modes of cultural integration.

The research confirms an increase in inter-communal tensions during the summer marching season: both communities reported increases in violence perpetrated by youths, the security forces and members of the 'other' religion. These findings suggest that individuals from Ardoyne are more likely to be both victims of physical attacks outside their area and/or by the security forces. The study concludes that high levels of fear cause residents to forego employment opportunities and education due to an inability to locate facilities in a perceived ' safe' environment. The costs related to this fear are undeniable, for both local business and leisure centres. The report stresses the importance of reducing fear by strategic investments to encourage normalised patterns of living.

70. Shirlow, Peter; Murtagh, Brendan; Mesev, Victor and McMullan, A. (2002) *Measuring and Visualising Labour Market and Community Segregation: A Pilot Study.* **Coleraine, University of Ulster.**

The study examines the community background and social class of individuals who work in mixed and segregated working environments. The report looks at the complexity of religious segregation and assimilation in the workplace. The research results indicate that the location of facilities within perceived 'safe' areas stimulates ethno-religious mixing. The findings explore the willingness of people from highly segregated communities with high levels of benefit dependency to work in mixed environments and suggest that the creation of neutral spaces would be likely to stimulate the employment of those from deprived areas. The study further suggests that workplace segregation impacts negatively upon many 'middle class' people from segregated areas. Citing this evidence, the report speculates that, under certain circumstances, workplace sectarianism may not be as prevalent as previously assumed.

The report suggests that residents of highly segregated and deprived areas are extremely conscious of locating 'safe' places to live and work. The majority of surveyed workers were found to live in segregated areas. Catholic workers were found to live in areas both increasingly deprived and closer to interfaces than their Protestant counterparts. The research suggests that disparities in social class composition between predominantly Protestant and Catholic communities may reflect the overall link between segregation and employment and the relationship between religion, skills, qualifications and social class.

Of the workplaces examined, those that maintain a mixed composition were more than five times more likely to employ residents from benefit-dependent and highly segregated communities. The segregated workplaces surveyed were six times less likely to draw workers from benefit-dependent communities. The location of employment was found to be more important than the frictional effects of distance. The research identified a general problem in relation to the uptake of work among those from areas of high dependency. The overall conclusion from the workplace survey is that greater mixing and the ability to locate work via 'safe' journeys could increase the number of mixed workplaces.

The report goes on to analyse the dissimilar ethnic profile of communities in Belfast, and the subsequent effects on local consumption. The research establishes that both Protestant and Catholic communities feel discriminated against when seeking employment. The majority of community residents surveyed indicated that their job seeking is influenced by fear, and that they remain unwilling to work in a workplace 'dominated' by the 'other' or in the 'other's' territory. The report argues that segregation may be more influential than sectarian animosity regarding employment decisions.

The research on the shopping and consumption patterns of interface communities reveals that despite spatial and socio-economic similarities, the two communities rarely share the majority of nearby services and facilities. The study examines attitudes of sectarian and non-sectarian individuals. Notably, those who held sectarian attitudes described their local interface communities in utopian terms, while non-sectarians were more likely to distinguish deviant behaviour, litter and other local problems. The section also discusses intra-community influences that perpetuate cross-community hostility and isolationism.

The final section of the report addresses policy implications regarding mixed workplaces. The research reports most policy implications to be rhetorical and that these fail to address the realities of community life. The study argues that planning has typically avoided the spatial effects of ethno-religious segregation, and invites responses which recognise indigenous employment needs within excluded areas and seek to connect local people with job opportunities both safely and efficiently.

71. Springfield Inter-Community Development Project (2000) *The Feud and the Fury.* **Belfast, SICDP.**

This report records the responses of the community sector while assisting families displaced during the Shankill feud. The publication aims to put in context the issues of displacement and consequential suffering of families. The research examines the chaotic response of the statutory sector to Belfast interface violence in 1996, and explores the subsequent policy changes implemented by statutory and community organisations. The study notes the importance of summer schemes, mobile phone networks and the Interagency Working Group for Displaced Families in diminishing community violence.

The research identifies the response of the Shankill community sector in accessing statutory funding resources for displaced families. The difficulty of maintaining neutrality is discussed. A list of complaints against the Housing Executive is included. The research identifies that a lack of coordination between statutory agencies contributed to the confusion of the situation. A theme of bureaucratic inefficiency from statutory agencies continues throughout the report.

The research analyses the effectiveness of the statutory sector and the Interagency Working Group on Displaced Families through a number of interviews with senior representatives. The North and West Belfast Health and Social Services Trust is attributed with considerable inaction, the community sector believes that the Trust failed to provide appropriate and user-friendly services for the victims of the feud, especially regarding counselling services. The report suggests that the Interagency Group, chaired by the North and West Trust, did not address Shankill concerns with sufficient urgency. The report includes the response of the Northern Ireland Housing Executive to the feud, and illustrates the success of NIHE's

amended procedures, designed to accommodate victims of the feud. The report is critical of the limited provisions available from the Social Security Agency, but concludes that changes to the social fund scheme cannot be made without significant alterations to the expenditure by the Treasury.
The study concludes by summarising the lessons learned by all participants. Eleven recommendations are included, which address necessary changes in the statutory and community sectors, amendments to the community-statutory partnership and increased media responsibility.

72. Springfield Inter-Community Development Project (1998) *Report of a Series of Seminars.* **Newtownabbey, Island Publications.**

This publication is an edited version of seminars overseen by SICDP on the issues of anti-social behaviour, interface difficulties and marching rights. Each discussion was facilitated by a speaker and followed by open discussion.

Impact of the Shankill/Falls/Springfield Interface: Brendan Murtagh spoke about the impact of walls upon communities and the 'costs' of living in a peace-line community. The problems of low income, deprivation, employment, education and limited access to resources were discussed. Chris O'Halloran of the Belfast Interface Project identified the three shared problems of all interface communities as social and economic disadvantage, ongoing violence and restricted access to facilities and services. Interface communities are unique from other deprived communities as they experience all three elements simultaneously. O'Halloran identifies shared community concerns as the role of young people in violence, restricted access, law and order issues and trauma problems. This research finds that the major factor which inhibits cross-community dialogue is not sectarianism, but people's fear of how they will be perceived within their own community. The plenary discussion covered numerous topics including the removal of the peace wall, ways of minimising tension, feelings of powerlessness within the community, the importance of confidence-building measures and problems with politicians.

Anti-Social Behaviour: Jim McCorry spoke about the community response to anti-social behaviour, the history of community policing and argued that communities must find a new way to address these issues. Tom Winston stressed the importance of community reconciliation, and outlined the format and structure of the proposed Alternatives programme. This system would be based on the merits of restorative justice. Michael Brown of Sinn Fein put the problem of community policing and punishment beatings in a political perspective. He acknowledged that the lack of Nationalist relations with the RUC has given rise to punishment beatings and re-affirmed support for restorative justice programmes and the role of a Community Charter as another preventative measure. Kieran McEvoy argued that, even if the RUC was perfect, there was still a need for a community-based restorative justice programme to effectively tackle criminal behaviour. He outlined his proposal for a restorative justice programme, which would meet the needs of victims, offenders and the community. The plenary session covered many relevant topics, including the successes and limitations of restorative justice schemes, the failings of previous initiatives, and potential links with the criminal justice system.

Young people at the Hatfield Community Centre held a supplementary discussion on the topic of anti-social behaviour. They debated the merits of the punishment-beating system, and the role of young women in anti-social behaviour. The group concluded that criminal activity is complex and that punishment beatings are an ineffective deterrent. The young people reported concerns about the involvement of paramilitaries in the restorative justice schemes, and remained sceptical that talking could solve criminal-behaviour problems.

Marching and Rights: Neil Jarman talked about the contentious issues of parading rights in several different countries and provided case studies from America, Israel and South Africa. Jarman concluded that people have neither an unlimited right to walk, nor an unlimited right to protest. The talk found that people who felt their rights were repressed by parades often reached some form of accommodation that acknowledged the diversity of human rights. The discussion then addressed the recent increase in contentious parades. Participants acknowledged Sinn Fein's role in organising protests, the non-publicity of negotiated, peaceful parading agreements and the difficulty of engaging with parade/protest leaders.

73. Springfield Inter-Community Development Project (1993) *Life on the Interface.* **Newtownabbey, Island Publications.**

This is a report of a conference of community groups regarding interface issues and their effects upon communities. The report begins with personal accounts of deprivation in local areas and presents joint suggestions for addressing shared socio-economic problems. The ongoing community violence is cited as detrimental to the community's attitudes towards shared facilities. The participants discuss a number of broad issues, including unemployment, social deprivation, youth alienation and local crime. The Government's Action for Community Employment (ACE) Programmes are criticised as unable to meet community needs and problems surrounding political vetting and community-group funding are raised. The topic of cross-community relations, and the subsequent lack of trust between communities, is discussed. The participants agree that interface areas require long-term regeneration programmes.

The plenary discussions revealed many different views and observations. Community safety issues and paramilitary threats were raised by a number of individuals. Most individuals reported feeling positive that communities could unite on health issues, unemployment, and housing. However, there was agreement that sectarianism had to be tackled before communities could move forward.

74. Smyth, Marie (ed) (1996) *Life in Two Enclave Areas in Northern Ireland.* **Derry, Templegrove Action Research Limited.**

This report investigates life experiences and daily routines of residents in the Catholic Gobnascale and the Protestant Fountain enclaves of Derry Londonderry. The research specifically examines post-ceasefire development within enclave areas and examines the effects of 'Troubles' related violence upon residents' decisions to either remain in the enclave area or relocate. The research compares current levels of economic activity with data from the 1991 Northern Ireland Census. It is found that both areas suffer from high deprivation, marginalisation and benefit dependency. The research analyses the migration patterns from both enclaves and examines the 'Troubles' related factors that influenced residential relocation. Gobnascale residents were found to have significantly more violence related factors that have affected migration decisions. The attitudes towards security between Fountain and Gobnascale residents were found to be vastly different.

The study analyses the impact of segregation upon the quality of life, and notes increasing patterns of residential segregation across the city. The report examines perceptions towards recent community change and future developmental projects for the two enclave areas. Similar levels of concern regarding local security and the environment are recorded in both areas. The research uncovers a significant difference between Gobnascale and Fountain residents regarding minority perception. A significant majority of Fountain residents identified themselves as a minority, while only a minority of Gobnascale residents maintained this perception. A near complete polarisation regarding political identity between the two areas was recorded. The research investigated local perceptions of major, minor, and past problems in each area. Both areas recorded unemployment as the most serious problem for the community. The report concludes that both areas remain acutely aware of a stigma perceived to be attached to their area. While differences emerge in terms of political affiliation and personal identity, similarities are recorded regarding unemployment and deprivation.

75. Smyth, Marie (ed) (1996) *Public Discussions on Aspects of Sectarian Division in Derry Londonderry.* **Derry, Templegrove Action Research Limited.**

This report includes findings from six public discussions held in Derry Londonderry on the aspects of sectarian division. The first public forum, entitled *The Name of the City*, presentes personal viewpoints by Anne Doherty and Alistair Wilson. Brian Wilson contributes a historical analysis of the numerous names for the area. The responses to the presentations yielded several critical letters from local residents. The section includes a proposal made by Templegrove Action Research for all political correspondence to be addressed as 'Derry Londonderry.' Contradictory responses to this proposal are included.

The second forum, *Is Segregation Desirable?*, incorporates the findings from the publication "Peace Line Communities: Implications for the Fountain" by Brendan Murtagh. The research concentrates on the deprivation faced by peaceline communities, and supports the maintenance of the wall around The Fountain. This presentation discusses the historical practice of residential segregation across Northern Ireland, and analyses the multiple deprivations within interface areas. The research provides psychological, practical and safety reasons for maintaining the barrier surrounding The Fountain.

The third forum, *Changing Population Balance and Protestant Drift*, includes 'Population Movement; The Statistics' by Marie Smyth, which addresses ongoing demographic change in Northern Ireland, which has experienced an increase in residential segregation. The research also examines internal migration patterns within the Derry Londonderry urban area. The forum includes two theatre monologues regarding the human effects of population movement, and records the topics raised during small-group discussions.

The fourth forum, *Loyalism*, discusses the research findings of 'Loyalism in Northern Ireland' by David Holloway. The research examines contemporary loyalism and explores the political ideals of loyalist fringe parties. It addresses themes of working-class alienation and new forms of social democratic politics emerging from the Protestant working class. The report includes the responses to the presentation on the topics of working-class politics, social change and religious identity.

The fifth forum, *The Shankill and the Falls: The Minority Experiences of Two Communities in West Belfast*, explores shared experiences between these divided areas. The experiences and concerns of the Shankill are presented by Jackie Redpath of the Greater Shankill Development Agency while Gerry Doherty, of Lenadoon Community Forum, describes the hardships and concerns faced by Lenadoon residents. Both presentations emphasise the need for long term strategic funding to address poverty and deprivation.

The sixth forum, *The Effects of Violence*, presents research findings from "The Effects of Violence in Communities" by Andrew Hamilton, which explores the relationship between segregation and violence in Northern Ireland. Notably, the increased rise in residential segregation perpetuates untrue myths and perceptions about the 'other' community. The topics raised in small group discussion include sectarian movements of population, the effects of political violence, peace and the political settlement and future integration.

76. Smyth, Marie (1995) *Three Conference Papers on Aspects of Segregation and Division.* Derry, Templegrove Action Research Limited.

This study presents three pieces of research on sectarianism and segregation in Northern Ireland. The first paper Aspects of Sectarianism discusses new strategies for researching sectarianism in communities across Northern Ireland. Paper Two Borders within borders: material and ideological segregation as forms of resistance and social control examines the changing pattern of spatial segregation in Derry Londonderry over the past twenty years. The final paper Limitations on the Capacity of Citizenship in Post Cease-fires Northern Ireland introduces factors that have contributed to the limitations of active citizenship in Northern Ireland, and examines the long-term effects of political violence and segregation on political dynamics.

77. Smyth, Marie (1995) *Borders Within Borders: Material and Ideological Segregation as Forms of Resistance and Strategies of Control*. Derry, Templegrove Action Research Limited.

Borders Within Borders examines segregation, population shifts and spatial demographics in Derry Londonderry. The study focuses on residential segregation and examines recent evidence which suggests that residential division in urban areas is deepening. The study illustrates that continuing political violence in Northern Ireland limits meaningful dialogue across the community divide. The first section researches the overall decline of the Protestant population in the Derry Londonderry area, and the internal shift of the Protestant population from the west to the east of the city. These residential adjustments have increased segregation in the areas, and the overall trend in population movement is of Protestant residents leaving the urban area.

The next section examines enclave communities and concludes that this spatial arrangement has increased segregation. The sense of community within enclaves was found to enhance hostile relationships between residents. The reasons given for leaving enclave communities were bad quality housing and fear of 'bad' influences, while the reasons for remaining in enclaves included financial inability to leave the situation and proximity to family members. Segregation is described as a strategy employed by communities to manage the real threat of violence and to create a less threatening environment for residents. Although residents cite 'safety concerns' as a reason for remaining in enclave communities, these areas have experienced more than their proportional share of violence. Divisions between enclave residents often occur because of different political affiliations and level of paramilitary support. This study describes the two main positive functions of enclave living as an increased sense of safety, and the development of community culture and solidarity. However, segregated living was found to exacerbate conflict by increasing mutual ignorance and fostering stereotypes.

The final section discusses forms of sectarian segregation and concludes that segregation has a material/spatial aspect, which manifests itself as residential segregation, and an ideological aspect, which regulates identity management and imposes restrictions on discourse between different group members. Segregation can be used as a strategy or principle, which has both intended and unintended consequences. The study concludes that segregation exists as both a form of resistance and control, by resisting outside threats and controlling the living environment. The report examines the strength of enclave cohesion, which has been necessary for the survival of areas, as subsequently blocking to cross-community networking and community development. This mentality creates communities better able to resist, rather than adapt to, community change.

78. Smyth, Marie; Morrissey, Mike and Hamilton, Jennifer (2001) *Caring Through the Troubles: Health and Social Services in North and West Belfast.* Belfast, North and West Health and Social Services Trust.

Caring Through the Troubles investigates the impact of the Troubles on the delivery of health and social care in North and West Belfast. It confirms that wards with greater exposure to political violence, and especially those with extreme experiences of the Troubles, report negative perceptions regarding health. The Cost of the Troubles data, along with extensive qualitative research, is re-analysed to explore the personal and psychological and health problems for particular wards.

Section One: *Introduction: Health, Equality and Political Violence in Northern Ireland* examines the strain placed upon NHS resources by extensive political violence in Northern Ireland and confirms that substantial health differences continue to exist because of social class and deprivation. The North and West Belfast Health Trusts areas are found to suffer from high levels of social exclusion and subsequent health and social needs.

Section Two: *Have the Troubles Affected People's Health?* reports that many individuals suffered little physical harm but substantial emotional distress from the Troubles. Those reporting poor physical health are mostly found in highly conflicted local areas. The report proposes that the differences in health may be due to the Troubles, rather than outright deprivation. The exposure to political violence, along with the established correlation between poor health and deprivation, creates a substantial burden for local healthcare providers. The study summarises the disproportionate amount of sectarian violence that has occurred within the Belfast Urban Area over the past thirty years and establishes that two-thirds of all fatalities and numerous sectarian assassinations occurred in North and West Belfast.

Section Three: *The Level of Need for Health and Social Services in North and West Belfast* includes extensive qualitative data from healthcare providers working in the North and West Belfast area and discusses the existing violence, personal stress and the 'culture of silence'. The report proposes that the Troubles have complicated and compounded other social problems, such as alcoholism, drug use and anti-social behaviour because of economic deprivation and paramilitary influence. The inability of workers to counteract paramilitary control within an area is discussed.

Section Four: *Factors in Delivering Health and Social Services in North and West Belfast* references the difficulties of stigma, segregation and violence upon health workers. Segregation and restrictions upon mobility due to safety concerns make certain vital resources inaccessible. The report suggests that the Trusts have accepted the sectarian divide and contribute to reproducing it. Many workers reported that the health services were inadequate to meet the degree of deprivation. The report chronicles difficulties experienced by NHS workers regarding community conflict, personal threats and mobility restrictions. North and West Trust staff reported high levels of stress, tension and anxiety associated with their work.

Section Five: *Conclusions and Recommendations* notes that those with the greatest experience of political violence most commonly report poor personal health. The Troubles have been an additional complication to other social problems, which have harmed the entire community by limiting health and social service provisions. The report concludes by making twelve recommendations regarding NHS policy.

79. Todd, Helen (2002) *Young People in the Short Strand Speak Out.* Belfast, University of Ulster.

This research explores the issues and concerns of young people living in the Short Strand. The study uncovers themes of apathy, disaffection from education and training opportunities and high levels of drug and alcohol consumption among the participants. The report recommends engaging young people by assisting them to participate in decision-making processes alongside service providers and policy makers.

Section One: *Introduction* examines the complex needs of young people living in disadvantaged areas. The rationale behind researching Short Strand is attributed to the high deprivation, high unemployment and high levels of mental stress within the community, while sectarian violence exacerbates social, psychological and environmental difficulties.

Section Two: *Review of Relevant Literature* examines the legislation introduced to assist young people in deprived areas and finds the current political agenda and social service provision to be fragmented and inefficient. The study examines why these efforts are not producing effective results and considers that the approach taken to engage with issues affecting young people has failed to create a participative, joined-up decision making process.

Section Three: *Methodology* adopts an ethnographic model and qualitative approach for dealing with difficult topics. The research gathers data from three community groups: one of young people, another of young mothers and a third of mothers with teenage sons and daughters.

Section Four: *Findings and Discussion* examines the key themes that emerged from the research. Few young people expected to gain qualifications from their education. Many complained about teachers' attitudes towards Short Strand residents and a lack of parental involvement in the education process was noted. All the young people voiced expectations that they would receive financial assistance from their parents/guardians, and young mothers focused on child rearing, rather than actively seeking employment. Many young people described rioting as a diversionary and exciting activity. Limited opportunities existed for young people in their area, and standing around in streets was noted as the main diversionary activity. Regular public drinking was perceived as a normal occurrence in the area, and the limits imposed by paramilitaries upon hard drugs within the community were noted. Strong community and family ties were noted, along with concerns over rioting, vandalism and housing shortages. Regarding perceptions of violence, participants were fearful of the long-term effects of rioting upon community safety and young people. Sectarian violence was reported as a major part of life in the Short Strand and perceived as normal activity. A general sense of thinking about immediate issues, rather than long-term concerns was noted. A direct correlation between those who enjoyed education and expectations of a career was recorded. A lack of trust in authority, and loss of faith in social workers and police was indicated.

Section Five: *Recommendations for Further Work* proposes four recommendations for Short Strand residents: the development of peer research, to access disadvantaged youths not included in the study, was proposed, along with a participative network to create changes in the education system; the study also supported the involvement of young people in the Community Restorative Justice Project and the inclusion of young people in community decision-making.

Section Six: *Critical Reflection* expresses dissatisfaction regarding the researcher's inability to engage with the most marginalised young people in the community. The respondents' willingness to engage, and to profess expressions of optimism about changing their situation despite inherent difficulties, was noted.

80. **Williams, Sue and Williams, Steve (2002)** *Ardoyne Road Arbitration: Report and Recommendations.* **Belfast, Office of the First Minister and Deputy First Minister.**

The Ardoyne Road arbitration process was initiated to advise the First Minister and the Deputy First Minister on the 'way forward' regarding the proposed wall around 41-49 Ardoyne Road in relation to the Holy Cross dispute. The arbitration process intended to move away from fixed positions held by Ardoyne residents and the Concerned Residents of Upper Ardoyne (CRUA) and find a solution that met the essential needs of all areas. The Ardoyne Road arbitration was not considered to be binding, but to act as an impartial recommendation to the First Minister and Deputy First Minister.

The report describes the violent history of the Ardoyne Road / Alliance Avenue interface. Both communities acknowledged that meeting safety needs required changing behaviours and attitudes within and between communities. This change will require dialogue in order to improve local community relations. The arbitrators emphasise the importance of community safety and community dialogue, as necessary to resolve the problem.

The arbitration recommends a three-pronged plan. First, the First Minister and the Deputy First Minister should address the basic safety needs by implementing the Minimal Wall/Fence Proposal. Next, attempts should be made to build confidence and dialogue between the communities. Finally, the recommendations advocate a process to gather local consensus on further improvements regarding community safety and the local environment.

There were several unsuccessful attempts by OFMDFM to resolve the dispute through both mediation and negotiation. The decision to pursue an option which incorporated traffic re-alignments and a barrier at the intersection of Ardoyne Road and Alliance Avenue, was welcomed enthusiastically by CRUA and rather reluctantly by the parents of the Lower Ardoyne. It was during these negotiations that CRUA ended their protest on the Ardoyne Road, and the Lower Ardoyne parents group increased membership by including all residents of Lower Ardoyne.

During the winter of 2002, community groups and OFMDFM struggled to incorporate community safety and community dialogue matters, with the lack of progress on one making it impossible to move on the other. By May 2003, there was little consensus between the Upper and Lower Ardoyne communities about a way forward with respect to addressing community safety needs. The arbitrators concurred that there was no consensus between the two communities regarding the proposed re-alignment and wall at the intersection. Without cross-community consent, it would not be possible for OFMDFM to proceed with certain aspects of the proposal.

The report attempts to 'unpack the reasoning' and clarify the needs, perceptions and opinions of the two communities regarding community safety. The need to prevent rioting and protect interface housing while providing a safe route for children travelling to school are strongly identified. The basic needs of the area, identified as the protection of life and property, are general security concerns and dealt with according to a security assessment made by the Police Service, which adjudged that there was no need for a 'peace wall' to protect 41-49 Ardoyne Road. The research also addresses the changing residential demographics of the area and relevant implications upon available housing. Concerns over rewarding violence and the erosion of public space are discussed. The report concludes by proposing interim measures to improve the perception of safety, which would include the provision of fencing for 41-49 Ardoyne Road.

81. Woodvale Resource Centre (1998) *Report on the Ardoyne-Springfield Interface.* **Belfast, Woodvale Resource Centre.**

This research examines attitudes of young people towards interface violence and recreational activities. The work questions the role of young people in perpetrating low-level violence across the 'peace lines'. Observations indicate that groups who did not live in the immediate area committed many stone-throwing incidents. The research aims to provide a better insight into the problems that affect local young people. The research found that a mixture of sectarianism, boredom and excitement motivated stone throwing and that 'peace lines' remain the most popular place for young people to meet up. The research also examines attitudes towards drinking, drug use, policing and paramilitary activity in the local area and concludes by cross-tabulating questions by age and gender.

82. Working Group on Peacelines (1994) *Report*. Belfast, NIO.

This report identifies sectarian divisions within the Belfast Urban Area, potential barriers for eventual removal and explores ways to make existing barriers more environmentally acceptable. The study was based upon qualitative community analysis. The report reviews community perceptions towards security barriers, noting that such barriers pose massive environmental problems, including dereliction of the local area. The study concludes that removal of these barriers is not a short or medium term option.

The report examines the fifteen existing barriers and the subsequent effects upon local communities. It establishes that many residents prefer segregated living for safety and identity reasons. The contrasting housing and population profile was found to increase peaceline problems. Although the report examines different options for land usage, it advocates a cautious approach to community relations work and housing policy. The report contains a detailed report of each interface community and presents financial regeneration proposals for three areas.

Publications in Chronological Order

1976
Boal, Frederick; Murray, R.C. and Poole Michael (1976) *Belfast: The Urban Encapsulation of a National Conflict.*

1982
Boal, Frederick (1982) *Segregating and Mixing: Space and Residence in Belfast.*

1985
Keane, Margaret Christine (1985) *Ethnic Residential Change in Belfast 1969-1977: The Impact of Public Housing Policy in a Plural Society.*

1993
Springfield Inter-Community Development (1993) *Project Life on the Interface.*

1994
Ballynafeigh Community Development Association (1994) *A Study of Attitudes to Community Relations in a Mixed Area of Belfast.*
Birrell, Derek (1994) *Social Policy Responses to Urban Violence in Northern Ireland.*
Boyes, Kevin and Quinn, Frankie (1994) *Interface Images.*
Bryson, Lucy and McCartney, Clem (1994) *Clashing Symbols? A Report on the Use of Flags, Anthems and Other National Symbols in Northern Ireland.*
Hepburn, A.C. (1994) *Long Divisions and Ethnic Conflict: The Experiences of Belfast.*
Murtagh, Brendan (1994) *Ethnic Space and the Challenge to Land Use Planning: A Survey of Belfast's Peace Lines.*
Working Group on Peacelines (1994) *Report.*

1995
Boal, Frederick (1995) *Shaping a City: Belfast in the Late Twentieth Century.*
Buckley, Anthony D. and Kenney, Mary Catherine (1995) *Urban Spaces, Violence and Identity in North Belfast.*
Doherty, Paul and Poole, Michael (1995) *Ethnic Residential Segregation in Belfast.*
Murtagh, Brendan (1995) *Image Making Versus Reality: Ethnic Division and the Planning Challenge of Belfast's Peace Lines.*
Neill, William J.V. (1995) *Lipstick on the gorilla? Conflict management, urban development and image making in Belfast.*

Smyth, Marie (1995) *Borders Within Borders: Material and Ideological Segregation as Forms of Resistance and Strategies of Control.*
Smyth, Marie (1995) *Three Conference Papers on Aspects of Segregation and Division.*

1996
Darby, John (1996) *Intimidation and the Control of Conflict in Northern Ireland.*
Moore, Ruth and Smyth, Marie (1996) *Two Policy Papers: Policing and Sectarian Division; Urban Regeneration and Sectarian Division.*
Smyth, Marie (ed) (1996) *Life in Two Enclave Areas in Northern Ireland.*
Smyth, Marie (ed) (1996) *Public Discussions on Aspects of Sectarian Division in Derry Londonderry.*

1997
Jarman, Neil (ed) (1997) *On The Edge: Community Perspectives on Civil Disturbances in North Belfast June-September 1996.*

1998
Belfast Interface Project (1998) *Interface Communities and the Peace Process.*
Belfast Interface Project (1998) *Young People on the Interface.*
Bollens, Scott A. (1998) *Urban Peace-Building in Divided Societies: Belfast and Johannesburg.*
Neill, William J.V. (1998) *Whose City? Can a Place Vision for Belfast Avoid the Issue of Identity?*
Shirlow, Peter (1998) *Fear, Mobility and Living in the Ardoyne and Upper Ardoyne.*
Springfield Inter-Community Development Project (1998) *Report of a Series of Seminars.*
Woodvale Resource Centre (1998) *Report on the Ardoyne-Springfield Interface.*

1999
Belfast Interface Project (1999) *Inner East Outer West.*
Bryan, Dominic and Jarman, Neil (1999) *Independent Intervention: Monitoring the Police, Parades and Public Order.*
Connolly, Paul and Maginn, Paul (1999) *Sectarianism, Children and Community Relations in Northern Ireland.*
Fay, Marie Therese; Morrissey, Mike; Smyth, Marie and Wong, Tracy (1999) *The Cost of the Troubles Study.*
Garvaghy Residents (1999) *Garvaghy: A Community Under Siege.*

Hall, Michael (ed) (1999) *Living in a Mixed Community: The Experiences of Ballynafeigh.*
Jarman, Neil (1999) *Drawing Back from the Edge: Community Based Responses to Violence in North Belfast.*
Murtagh, Brendan (1999) *Community and Conflict in Rural Ulster.*

2000
Bollens, Scott A. (2000) *On Narrow Ground: Urban Policy and Ethnic Conflict in Jerusalem and Belfast.*
Ellis, Geraint and McKay, Stephen (2000) *City Management Profile Belfast.*
Gallagher, Ryan (ed) (2000) *BT5: A Photographic Exploration of Identity by Young People in East Belfast.*
Jarman, Neil and O'Halloran, Chris (2000) *Peacelines or Battlefields: Responding to Violence in Interface Areas.*
Northern Ireland Housing Executive (2000) *The North Belfast Housing Strategy: Tackling Housing Needs.*
Springfield Inter-Community Development Project (2000) *The Feud and the Fury.*

2001
Community Dialogue (2001) *North Belfast: Where Are We At?*
East Belfast Community Development Agency (2001) *Leading from Behind: An Agenda for Change in East Belfast.*
Forthspring Inter-Community Group and Belfast Exposed (2001) *The Hurt, the Peace, the Love and the War.*
Gaffikin, Frank; McEldowney, Malachy and Sterrett, Ken (2001) *Remaking the City: The Role of Culture in Belfast, in Urban planning and Cultural Inclusion: Lessons from Belfast and Berlin.*
Hall, Michael (ed) (2001) *Community Relations: An Elusive Concept.*
Hall, Michael (ed) (2001) *Young People Speak Out: Newhill Youth Development Team.*
Hamilton, Michael (2001) *Working Relationships: An Evaluation of Community Mobile Phone Networks in Northern Ireland.*
McEldowney, Malachy; Sterrett, Ken and Gaffikin Frank (2001) *Architectural Ambivalence: the Built Environment and Cultural Identity in Belfast.*
Officer, David (2001) *Towards a Community Relations Strategy for Donegall Pass.*
Shirlow, Peter (2001) *Fear and Ethnic Division*
Smyth, Marie; Morrissey, Mike and Hamilton, Jennifer (2001) *Caring Through the Troubles: Health and Social Services in North and West Belfast.*

2002
Bill, Anne (2002) *Beyond the Red Gauntlet.*
Hall, Michael (ed) (2002) *Reuniting the Shankill: A Report on the Greater Shankill Community Exhibition and Convention.*
Hall, Michael (ed) (2002) *An Uncertain Future: An Exploration by Protestant Community Activists.*
Henry, Pat; Hawthorne, Isy; McCready, Sam and Campbell, Hugh (2002) *The Summer of 2002: An evaluation of the impact of diversionary funding for work with young people in Belfast interfaces during the summer of 2002.*
Jarman, Neil (2002) *Managing Disorder: Responses to Interface Violence in North Belfast.*
Murtagh, Brendan (2002) *The Politics of Territory: Policy and Segregation in Northern Ireland.*
North Belfast Community Action Project (2002) *Report of the Project Team.*
Robinson, Peter (2002) *Victims: The Story of Unionists 'Living' at the Interface with Republican Short Strand.*
Shirlow, Peter; Murtagh, Brendan; Mesev, Victor and McMullan, A. (2002) *Measuring and Visualising Labour Market and Community Segregation: A Pilot Study.*
Todd, Helen (2002) *Young People in the Short Strand Speak Out*
Williams, Sue and Williams Steve (2002) *Ardoyne Road Arbitration: Report and Recommendations.*

2003
Basten, Anne and Lysaght, Karen (2003) *Violence, Fear and 'the everyday': Negotiating Spatial Practices in the City of Belfast.*
Hall, Michael (ed) (2003) *Beginning a Debate: An Exploration by Ardoyne Community Activists.*
Hall, Michael (ed) (2003) *The East Belfast Interface (1): Lower Newtownards Youth Speak Out.*
Hall, Michael (ed) (2003) *The East Belfast Interface (2): Short Strand Youth Speak Out.*
Hall, Michael (ed) (2003) *It's Good to Talk: The Experiences of the Springfield Mobile Phone Network.*
Kuusisto-Arponen, Anna-Kaisa (2003) *Our Places - Their Spaces.*
Lenadoon Community Forum (2003) *Lenadoon Community Forum, 1992-2002.*

2004

Ballymurphy Women's Centre (2004) *Women on the Edge: Conference Report*.
Belfast Interface Project (2004) *A Policy Agenda for the Interface*.
Cadwallader, Anne (2004) *Holy Cross: The Untold Story*.
Hall, Michael (ed) (2004) *Exploring the Marching Issue: Views from Nationalist North Belfast*.
Heatley, Colm (2004) *Interface: Flashpoints in Northern Ireland*.
Inter-Action Belfast (2004) *Strategic Plan 2004-2007*.
Persic, Callie (2004) *The State of Play*.

2005

Hall Michael (ed) (2005) *Finding Common Ground: An Exploration by Young People from Both Sides of the East Belfast Interface*.
Jarman, Neil (2005) *Demography, Development and Disorder: Changing Patterns of Interface Areas*.

Index

Children and Young People: 7, 12, 31, 34, 35, 37, 40, 41, 44, 51, 66, 72, 79, and 81

Community Development: 20, 37, 54, 56, 65, 71, 72, and 75

Community Relations: 3, 39, 41, 43, 46, 60, 65, and 77

Community Safety: 1, 42, 69, and 73

Community Violence: 2, 4, 5, 7, 8, 12, 18, 19, 22, 26, 30, 31, 32, 33, 34, 35, 36, 40, 43, 47, 48, 48, 49, 50, 51, 53, 63, 67, 72, 78, 79 and 81

Cross-Community Work: 21, 29, 31, 40, 53, and 73

Demographic Change: 24, 45, 47, and 75

Deprivation: 4, 6, 7, 13, 14, 15, 26, 27, 33, 34, 35, 38, 39, 54, 59, 60, 63, 65, 66, 68, 70, 73, 74, and 79

Healthcare: 78

History: 10, 11, 14, 17, 22, 23, 45, 55, and 61

Holy Cross: 8, 19, 38, and 80

Housing: 52, 57, 62, and 64

Mediation: 5 and 80

Mixed Residential Areas: 1 and 41

Mobile Phone Networks: 36, 42, and 49

Parades: 16, 30, 32, 44, 50, 51, and 72

Photography: 15, 27, and 29

Policing: 16, 37 and 56

Policy Recommendations: 2, 4, 6, 24, 42, 44, 46, 47, 48, 49, 50, 51, 55, 58, 59, 62, 63 and 71

Politics: 8, 9, 12, 19, 25, 38, 39, 48, 61, 67, 76, and 80

Residential Segregation: 3, 5, 10, 11, 12, 18, 20, 22, 23, 33, 45, 48, 52, 53, 56, 57, 58, 60, 64, 66, 68, 69, 74, 75, 76, 77 and 82

Rural Planning: 58

Spatial Practices: 3, 60, 68, 69, 70, 74, 76 and 77

Trauma: 19, 26 and 78

Urban Planning: 6, 9, 10, 13, 14, 17, 18, 25, 28, 55, 57, 59, 60, 61, 62, 64 and

Urban Regeneration: 25 and 28

Workplace Segregation: 70.

ICR REPORTS

The following is a full list of the research reports that have been produced by ICR. Wherever possible reports are made available on our website, some however remain the property of the commissioning body and are retained as internal documents.

New Migrant Communities in East Tyrone. Jennifer Betts and Jennifer Hamilton, (2005) Commissioned by East Tyrone College of Further and Higher Education.

No Longer a Problem: Sectarian Violence in Northern Ireland. Neil Jarman, (2005) Commissioned by Office of the First Minister and Deputy First Minister.

Ballysillan Residents' Attitudes towards Church Participation, Community Involvement and Neighbourhood Safety. Mary Conway, (2005). Ballysillan Bridgebuilding Forum and ICR.

Young People's Attitudes and Experiences of Policing, Violence and Community Safety in North Belfast. Jonny Byrne, Mary Conway and Malcolm Ostermeyer, (2005). Commissioned by the Northern Ireland Policing Board.

Young People in Community Conflict. Jonny Byrne, Jennifer Hamilton and Ulf Hansson, (2005). Commissioned by Northern Health and Social Services Board.

Sectarian and Racist Chill Factors in Armagh College. Jennifer Hamilton, (2005). Commissioned by Armagh College of Further and Higher Education.

Community Cohesion: Applying Learning from Groundwork in Northern Ireland. Neil Jarman, Libby Keyes, Jenny Pearce and Derick Wilson, (2004) Commissioned by Groundwork UK.

Sectarianism in Armagh City and District Council Area. Jennifer Hamilton, (2004) Commissioned by Community Relations Council.

Out of Sight: Young People and Paramilitary Exiling in Northern Ireland. Jonny Byrne, (2004). Commissioned by Save the Children and NIACRO.

Report on the Consultation about proposals for a Chinese Community Centre on Donegall Pass, Belfast. Neil Jarman, (2004). Commissioned by Belfast City Council.

Community Relations, Community Cohesion and Regeneration: A training and development strategy for Groundwork Northern Ireland. Neil Jarman and Paul Hutchinson, (2004). Commissioned by Groundwork NI.

Young People in the Greater Shantallow Area. Ulf Hansson, (2004). Off the Streets and ICR.

Sectarianism in the Limavady Borough Council Area. Jonny Byrne, (2004). Commissioned by Community Relations Council.

Mediation Northern Ireland Policing Project: Interim Evaluation. Neil Jarman, (2004). Commissioned by Mediation Northern Ireland.

Demography, Development and Disorder: Changing Patterns of Interface Areas. Neil Jarman, (2004). Commissioned by Community Relations Council.

Crime – A Waste of Time. Crime and Anti-Social Behaviour in Sunningdale. Fabrice Mourlon and Ulf Hansson, (2004). North Belfast Alternatives and ICR.

Evaluation Report of Diversity Challenges. Ruth Moore, Brandon Hamber and Neil Jarman, (2004). Commissioned by Diversity Challenges.

Sectarianism in the Antrim Borough Council Area. Jonny Byrne, (2004). Commissioned by Community Relations Council.

Sectarianism in the Larne District Council Area. Jonny Byrne, (2004). Commissioned by Community Relations Council.

Legislative Provisions for Hate Crime across EU Member States. Rebecca Thomas, (2004). ICR.

Migrant Workers in Northern Ireland. Kathryn Bell, Neil Jarman and Thomas Lefebvre, (2004). Commissioned by the Office of the First Minister and Deputy First Minister.

Racist Harassment in Northern Ireland. Neil Jarman and Rachel Monaghan, (2004). Commissioned by the Office of the First Minister and Deputy First Minister.

Young People's Attitudes and Experiences of Sectarianism and Community Conflict in Larne. Jonny Byrne, (2004). Commissioned by YMCA.

The Impact of Political Conflict on Children in Northern Ireland. Marie Smyth with Marie Therese Fay, Emily Brough and Jennifer Hamilton, (2004). ICR.

A Review of the Health and Social Care Needs of Victims/Survivors of the Northern Ireland Conflict. Jennifer Hamilton, Jonny Byrne and Neil Jarman, (2003). Commissioned by Eastern Health and Social Services Board.

An Acceptable Prejudice? Homophobic Violence and Harassment in Northern Ireland. Neil Jarman and Alex Tennant, (2003). Commissioned by the Office of the First Minister and Deputy First Minister.

Young People and Politics. North Belfast Community Research Group, (2003). LINC Resource Centre and ICR.

Policing, Accountability and Young People. Jennifer Hamilton, Katy Radford and Neil Jarman, (2003). Commissioned by Office of the Police Ombudsman for Northern Ireland and Northern Ireland Policing Board.

Analysis of Incidents of Racial Harassment Recorded by the Police in Northern Ireland. Neil Jarman and Rachel Monaghan, (2003). Commissioned by the Office of the First Minister and Deputy First Minister.

Human Rights and Community Relations: Competing or Complimentary Approaches in Response to Conflict? Neil Jarman (ed), (2002). ICR.

The Human Impact of the Troubles on Housing Provision and Policy. Jennifer Hamilton, Rachel Monaghan and Marie Smyth, (2002). Commissioned by Northern Ireland Housing Executive.

Creggan Community Restorative Justice: An Evaluation and Suggested Way Forward. Marie Smyth, Jennifer Hamilton and Kirsten Thomson, (2002). ICR and St Columb's Park House.

Caring Through the Troubles: Health and Social Services in North and West Belfast. Marie Smyth, Mike Morrissey and Jennifer Hamilton, (2001). Commissioned by North and West Health and Social Services Board.

Reviewing REAL Provision: An Evaluation of Provision and Support for People Affected by the Northern Ireland Troubles. Jennifer Hamilton, Kirsten Thomson and Marie Smyth, (2001). Commissioned by Northern Ireland Voluntary Trust.